SAILS THROUGH THE CENTURIES

SAILS THROUGH THE CENTURIES

BY SAM SVENSSON

ILLUSTRATIONS BY GORDON MACFIE

The Macmillan Company, New York ⟪ Collier-Macmillan Ltd., London

CONTENTS

PREFACE

This illustrated book is the result of close cooperation between author and artist. All the drawings were made before the text was written, the artist obtaining his material from several sources: his own sketches based on personal observation, authenticated drawings, old models, and, in more recent times, actual photographs. To some extent it has been practicable to identify by name some of the vessels illustrated, and wherever possible the names are given. Vessels so identified can be regarded both as characteristic of their type and as correct in detail for the particular ship illustrated.

The presentation is, on the whole, chronological, and the reader's attention is first called to earlier types of vessels. It has not been found possible, however, to adhere entirely to chronological order, as typographical considerations have necessarily had an influence on the sequence. Because more information is available for the nineteenth century, this work contains numerous examples from that period.

The artist, Gordon Macfie, was born on the west coast of Sweden, and since childhood, he has observed and studied a wide variety of ships. Working in the medium of pen and brush, he has demonstrated his love for his subject, and all the illustrations reveal superb artistry as well as every consideration for accuracy of detail.

All the illustrations are referred to in the text, which, though it is somewhat technical in nature, may be easily understood when reference is made to the relevant illustration. The text shows how the various types of vessels developed, and it also gives the reader both a general historical background and a brief history of those vessels that are identified by name.

Since ancient times, the two most common methods of fastening planking to the hulls of wooden craft have been carvel and clinker. In the carvel-built boat, the planks are laid flush alongside one another, which results in a smooth surface; in the clinker method, the planks overlap, the side of the craft thus being stepped. The smooth carvel method has its origin in the Mediterranean, where as early as classical times, large ships were carvel-built. Owing to the shortage of suitable long lengths of timber, small pieces of wood had to be used, and they were joined in such an ingenious way that they provided tight, strong planking. From the eastern Mediterranean the carvel-built method spread to Western and Northern Europe. The method and stages by which it spread are largely unknown.

Figure 1 shows a Roman merchantman, circa A.D. 200, copied from a marble relief that was found in Ostia, Rome's ancient seaport. The vessel is carvel-built and is navigated by two steering oars, one on each quarter, and she has two masts. The foremast slants steeply over the bow and carries a single sail called the "artemon." The mainmast carries a large square sail with two small topsails above. The mainsail is adorned with the allegorical figures of Romulus and Remus.

The Roman ship could not sail by the wind and had to remain in port until the wind was suitable, or "fair," which is the usual expression used by sailors. In a storm the high stern was turned toward the sea and the vessel drifted before the wind. Vessels of this type could have been fairly large, for there is a report of a Roman ship that was 180 feet long. In the twenty-seventh chapter of the Acts of the Apostles, a description is given of Paul's voyage to Rome in a ship having 276 persons on board. When, during this voyage, they had to anchor near Malta for fear of going on the rocks, they anchored from the stern, so that the ship's low head was turned away from the sea. At dawn they threw the cargo of wheat overboard in order to lighten the ship, loosened the rudder bands, hoisted the artemon, and made toward a sandy beach to try to save their lives. Perhaps Paul's ship was of the same type as the vessel from Ostia.

Clinker construction was developed on the Baltic. At the time of the Vikings, it had reached a high degree of craftsmanship. Their ships were double-ended, built of oak, had no decks, and were navigated with a steering oar, which was placed on the right-hand side of the hull, near the stern. This side was therefore called "steerboard," a name that long ago came to be pronounced *"star*board" and as such is used internationally to this day. During the Viking Age, there were several different types of ships—men-of-war that were rowed and sailed, merchantmen that depended almost entirely upon sail. The rig was simple but effective. The mast stood almost amidships, which made the vessels exceedingly maneuverable; and with their single square sail, the ships of the Viking Age could sail with the wind abeam.

The large men-of-war were called "longships," the smaller ones *snacker* or *karvar*. Figure 2 shows such a small man-of-war, which in its main essentials is a copy of the Norwegian Gokstad ship. This ship, not a seagoing craft, is an intermediate size called a *karvi* and was found in the year 1880 in a burial mound near Sandefjord. It is now kept in a museum at Oslo. Its dimensions are: length, 77 feet; beam, 17 feet; and depth, almost 6 feet. The draft is estimated at 3.6 feet, which would give a displacement of about 22 tons. It is believed that the sail was 750 square feet in area and was set and trimmed by halyards, braces, tacks, and sheets. Instead of a bowline, a rope that pulls the weather edge of the sail forward, the navigators of this ship used a pole, the so-called *beitås*. This pole may also have been set against the weather leech of the sail to tauten it ahead and give the vessel greater ability to point closer to the wind.

The small cargo boats of the Viking Age were called *byrdingar,* a word related to "burden." They were used for trading in home waters and for victualing the longships, which could not carry on board all the supplies necessary for their large crews. The large merchantmen were called *knarrar*. They were shorter, broader, and more seaworthy than the longships. The *knarr* was used for longer voyages—to Iceland and Greenland.

At the end of the Viking Era and at the beginning of the Middle Ages, new types of vessels appeared; or, more correctly, the existing types changed through influences from Western and Southern Europe. The *cog* was such a type and is believed to have its origin in Friesland or Flanders. With the appearance of Western European shipping and the Hanseatic League, the cog became more common at the expense of the Nordic types of ships. As sea warfare at that time consisted largely in hand-to-hand fighting between the crews, the higher ships enjoyed a tactical advantage over the lower, and this led to the building of "castles" (battle platforms) at each end of ships. Even the merchantman was fitted out in this way, because it was always necessary for the seafarer to be able to defend himself. The first time a castle is mentioned in connection with a Nordic ship is in the saga of Håkan Hårdabred (1157-1161). In the battle at Nordre River, near Göteborg, against King Inge, Håkan had two Baltic traders in his fleet fitted out with a castle at the stem as well as the masthead.

Figure 3 shows a *knarr* or an early cog copied from a picture on an old seal. The ship still has a steering oar, and built-up castles fore and aft, as well as a fighting top. In order to strengthen the ships, the deck beams were usually carried out through the planking and hooked over the planks, which prevented the sides from falling out. On the whole, the rig was similar to that of the Viking Era, but the sail had bowlines leading to a spar at the stem called the "bowsprit."

The single-masted rig was scarcely changed during the following centuries, and only in the second half of the fifteenth century did two or three masts become usual

in Northern Europe. The Mediterranean triangular lateen sail, which had moved along the coasts of Europe in the form of a mizzen, reached the Baltic at the end of the Middle ages and soon became common. The lateen sail was used as a mizzen because it could be trimmed to help the steering. The stern rudder was invented during the twelfth century, probably in Friesland, and gradually took the place of the Nordic steering oar. The oldest known depiction of a stern rudder is on a christening font in Winchester Cathedral and is believed to date from 1180.

The cog, which was the large ship during the Middle Ages, was used both for trade and in war, and she was gradually replaced by a stronger type, the *holk,* which became the most important type of ship in Northern Europe during the fifteenth century. Figure 4 shows a *holk* that dates from the end of the Middle Ages. The castles have developed into an integral part of the ship and are carvel-built on top of the clinker-built hull. The vessel still has a few beams carried through the planking to keep the sides of the ship together; outboard, there are vertical fenders, which protected the sides and the ends of the beams when the ship was tied up at dockside or facilitated handling boats or cargo.

The rig had become stabilized; the shrouds were rattled down, and fighting tops had become the rule. Additional sails called "bonnets" were substituted for reefs in the sails. The bonnet was a detachable part of the sail and was taken off when the sail had to be shortened in strong winds. The *holk* in the drawing, possibly one of the Hanseatic traders, has a deck cargo of dried fish and might be on her way from Bergen to Lübeck.

3

4

5b

5c

MACFIE

5a

The triangular lateen sail had been introduced in the Mediterranean by the Arabs in the eighth century, and from that time small ships and boats were rigged with such sails. In Spain and Portugal, these small carvel-built ships were called "caravels," while larger ships were known as *naos,* from the Latin *naves.* Columbus' SANTA MARIA was a *nao,* while the two accompanying vessels were caravels. One of these was called NINA *(The Small One),* the other PINTA *(The Painted One).* Figure 5 shows Columbus' fleet on his first voyage. No one knows, however, exactly what the ships looked like in detail. The large ship is built with a forecastle and a poop. She has three masts, with the middle mast dominating, in the style of the Middle Ages. The mainsail has two bonnets and a new type of buntline called a "martinet," lines that are fitted on both sides of the sail and effectively catch it under the yard when the yard is lowered. The ship also has a main topsail on a short yard; this sail is sheeted to the main yard in the manner that be-

came more common at a later date. She also has a sail under the bowsprit, the spritsail (in Dutch and in Middle English called *blinde* because it impaired visibility ahead).

The two caravels may be regarded as representative of their type. The small NINA was the fleet's best sailer and often led the way. She had only a lateen sail, while the PINTA had two square sails.

At the top of the mainmast, the SANTA MARIA carries the standard of Castile and León; on the foremast, the identification flag of the expedition, which bears a green cross and the initials of Isabella and Ferdinand. Portuguese men-of-war, shimmering in pale blue and pink, sail on the surface of the water and give an impression of tropical seas. Above is Toscanelli's chart, dated 1478, which shows India where America ought to be. It was this map that inspired Columbus to make the voyage, and all his life he believed that he had discovered India on his westward voyage.

The *carrack* is another type of ship whose origin can be traced to the Mediterranean but which was also found in Western Europe. She is believed to have been developed in Italy. During the fifteenth century, Genoa used carracks in trading with England. The oldest type had one mast, but after the middle of the century, they were three-masted. In Columbus' fleet, during his second voyage to America, in 1493, there were three carracks and several caravels.

Figure 6 shows a carrack from the beginning of the sixteenth century; the illustration was copied mainly from a stained-glass window in King's Chapel, Cambridge. It shows a broad, full-built ship, with a deep draft and high superstructures. The hull is carvel-built, with broad wales evenly distributed over the side of the ship and with the superstructure fore and aft built integrally with the hull. The three-masted rig has five sails—foresail, mainsail, mizzen, and two topsails. The three lower sails have one bonnet each. The two upper sails are small and were set and taken in by men aloft, the halyards, braces, and sheets being let into the top. Development took place in such a way that the masthead flag was turned into a sail without the flag itself disappearing. It was merely moved up above the new sail to inspire at a later date still another sail, the topgallant sail.

Ever since the middle of the fourteenth century, guns have been used on board ships. At first they were quite small and were placed on deck or in the castles so that the crew could fire scrap metal on enemy vessels. In 1501 a Frenchman named Descharges, from Brest, is said to have cut portholes in the sides of a ship and placed the guns on a second deck below the first; this in turn made the use of larger guns possible by keeping the heavier weight lower down, balancing the ship. With the advent of this innovation, more serious damage could be caused to hostile ships, which again led to larger and stronger ships being built. It was characteristic of the sixteenth century that all seafaring nations built one or two very large men-of-war.

The word "carvel" means either carvel-built or denotes a type of ship. It is philologically related to "caravel"; but except for the name and the fact of being carvel-built, these big ships had nothing in common with the Spanish caravels. The type of ship that is known in Western Europe as a "galleon" is regarded as being of the same type as the Swedish carvel. A striking detail in Figure 6 is that the protruding forecastle of the carrack has now become shorter and does not reach outside the stem. Instead, the head now has a lower protruding part, a beakhead, which was characteristic of the galleon and the carvel.

Figure 7 shows a large carvel or galleon from the middle of the sixteenth century. The hull depicted was reconstructed from various contemporary drawings, while the rig was modeled on that of the Swedish ELEFANTEN. As no reliable information is available except that the main measurements are those of the ELEFANTEN, it has not been found possible to reconstruct her hull with complete accuracy.

As shown in Figure 7, the topsails have now increased considerably in area, and the mainmast is fitted with a topmast, which was firmly lashed to the mast and so could not be struck. The mainsail is still larger than the foresail, and both have two bonnets, while the triangular lateen mizzen has only one. All the square sails are rigged with clew lines, and the lower sails are fitted with martinets, which were used to catch hold of the sail from both sides and pull it in under the yard when the yard was lowered and the sail was furled. The lower yardarms are equipped with grapnel cutters, intended to catch and sever the rigging of hostile ships. The ship has a spritsail under the bowsprit, and the mizzenmast carries a small lateen topsail. A flag with the Swedish cross had not yet come into use, but the pennant on the mainmast shows the three Swedish crowns.

MACFIE

8

MACFIE

9

MACFIE

10

8. *Large man-of-war, company ship, galleon, from the end of the sixteenth century*
9. *A boyart, a small Northern European sailing vessel from the sixteenth century*
10. *A flute (flyboat) with a round stern and bluff bow, a common Dutch merchantman during the seventeenth century*

In the late fifteenth century, some large ships began to be rigged with four masts, the two forward ones being square-rigged, while the two after ones usually were rigged with lateen sails. Figure 8 shows such a large ship, built about the end of the sixteenth century. Comparing it with the older ship in Figure 7, we can see that the forecastle and the beakhead have become lower, that a gallery has been built around the stern of the ship, and that rich decoration has been added.

The ship has one more square sail, a topgallant sail, pronounced "t'ga'n's'l," on the two square-rigged masts, and the masts have been divided into three parts, lower mast, topmast, and topgallant mast. The latter two could be struck, that is, rigged up and down (an invention of about 1570 that is attributed to the Dutch). A small pole, the jack staff, is rigged on the forward end of the bowsprit. All the head braces lead to the stays of the mainmast and down to the deck, and the main braces return to the mainmast. Unlike small barges and boats, the larger ships did not yet carry staysails.

Figure 9 shows a late-sixteenth-century small coaster with staysails. It was known as a *boyart* and was found in the North Sea and the Baltic. Mention was made of it in Sweden from the time of Gustavus Vasa until the end of the seventeenth century. It was the first ship with a true fore-and-aft sail. The *boyart* was carvel-built, with a round stern, and had accommodations aft, where the crew lived under a tent. Though the *boyart* was used for shipping small cargoes, vessels of this type were also used in the navy. The drawing shows her rigged with a fore-and-aft mainsail and forestaysail, a spritsail under the bowsprit, and a small lateen mizzen. Sometimes a square topsail was carried on a topmast; otherwise, the mainmast could be rigged only with square sails.

The Dutch dominated Northern European shipping for a long time, and Dutch shipbuilding was very active. Toward the end of the sixteenth century, a new type of ship was constructed in the town of Hoorn. It became known as the *flute,* or "flyboat." It was very narrow in relation to its length, with straight sides fore and aft, a very broad bow called "apple-cheeked," and a round stern. Like all Dutch ships, the *flute* had a shallow draft and a flat bottom. She sailed well, but with her narrow hull she was very cranky, and both spars and sails had to be of moderate dimensions. Because the rigging was light, the *flute* could be sailed by a small crew; this made her more economical to run.

Figure 10 shows an early-seventeenth-century Dutch *flute*. It is double-ended and has very full lines. Above the round stern appears a small transom with a lantern on an iron arm. The rig has only six sails—foresail and mainsail with topsails above, spritsail, and mizzen. This was the usual rig for small ships during the entire seventeenth century.

With its high stem, the ship of those days was apt to be very weatherly in a quartering wind, and there was a great need for headsails. At the beginning of the seventeenth century, large ships therefore rigged a spar, such as a topgallant mast, at the end of the bowsprit and there set a small square sail, called a "spritsail topsail." This rigging must have been very impractical, but the spritsail topsail was used for more than a century, which shows that there was a great need for a headsail.

As late as 1620, some large ships still had four masts, the two aft being rigged with lateen sails (see Figure 8). At that time, however, mariners began to rig the third mast with a square topsail above the mizzen. At about the same time, the fourth mast disappeared, and the new rig soon became international, all large ships thereafter having three masts with square sails on all of them. This rig became known as "ship rig," or "full rig," and for a long time it was regarded as the most distinguished rig of all sailing ships. The large men-of-war—the East Indiamen of the eighteenth century and the clippers of the nineteenth century—were ship-rigged.

At the beginning of the seventeenth century, a new type of ship appeared in Holland, the *pinnace*. The meaning of the name is quite different from that of a pinnace in modern English. It differed from the *flute* mainly in that it had a beakhead and a square transom. As a man-of-war, the pinnace could carry about twenty-four guns between decks. This type of vessel was later succeeded by the frigate, which became the fast-sailing medium-sized man-of-war of the eighteenth century. The pinnace was also used as a merchant ship for long voyages, and the KALMAR NYCKEL, the first Swedish ship that sailed over the Atlantic to New Sweden, was probably a ship of this type, though this cannot be substantiated.

Figure 11 shows a mid-seventeenth-century Dutch pinnace. The high forecastle has disappeared entirely, though the afterbody still remains high. The ship has a square stern, and above the transom is an allegorical picture giving the name of the ship. This was a common way of indicating the name, probably because of general illiteracy. The ship carries topgallant sails above the topsails, as well as spritsail, spritsail topsail, lateen mizzen, and mizzen topsail. The curtainlike martinets on the courses have by this time disappeared, but the lower courses still have bonnets. With the exception of the spritsail topsail and the mizzen topsail, the rigging has not changed to any great extent since the second half of the sixteenth century.

11

12

In addition to the large ships, there were many small ones of different types used for different purposes. At an early date, there were official ships; this was especially true in Holland, owing to the necessity of patrolling her canal system. Figure 12 shows such a Dutch yacht, from a drawing dated 1678. The word "yacht" is used here in its original meaning: a small craft of graceful lines often used in patrol or pursuit. Like all shallow-draft Dutch ships, it has so-called iceboards, one on each side, which were lowered on the leeward side when sailing by the wind in order to decrease leeway, in a manner similar to that of the centerboard of a sailing dinghy. The rigging of the yacht shows a gaff-mainsail without a boom, forestaysail, jib, and a topsail. The yard has no braces, though its sheets were led astern so that they could also serve as braces for the lower yard. The gaff is a new spar that, during the eighteenth century, was to take the place of the lateen yard in most ships. This completed the conversion of the lateen lugsail to the fore-and-aft sail.

Small ships were also used for other purposes. The Swedish postal department in days gone by attached great importance to mail vessels, which also carried passengers and light cargo. When Sweden held possessions on the other side of the Baltic, the traffic in these mail packets was fairly lively, and even at a later date the necessity of maintaining postal communication by sea remained.

Figure 13 shows a Swedish mail packet built at Karlskrona in 1692. She was called HIORTEN and cost 1,600 Swedish dalers. This sloop, together with several others, sailed between Ystad and Stralsund until 1702. Nowadays we should say that HIORTEN was rigged like a ketch, the mainmast forward and the mizzen stepped ahead of the rudderpost. A sloop today is any small boat with a single mast and headsail; originally, the word pertained to a vessel with only one deck. HIORTEN had a standing gaff-mainsail and a mizzen without booms. The sails were furled to the gaff and the mast through lines in the sail called "brails." The other sails were forestaysail, jib, and square topsail. It will be noted in Figure 13 that she has a small flag on a pole at the end of the gaff, and in the inventory of HIORTEN this is referred to as the "gaff flag." At the masthead, she flies a long pennant on a short gaff. At a much later date, this gaff was called a "monkey gaff," the word "monkey" being English nautical parlance for a small or insignificant feature.

13

MAGPIE

14

In the 1660's, large ships were gradually equipped with staysails. The first was a sail on the mainstay that was set only in bad weather, when most of the other sails were furled. Later a sail was added to the main-topmast stay, to the mizzen stay, and finally to the fore-topmast stay, so that by the end of the century, large ships carried these four staysails.

About the same time as the introduction of staysails, reefs were being introduced in square sails. A start was made with the topsails, which received one reef each, and toward the end of the century the lower sails also had reefs. Reefs required the sailor to work on the yards more frequently than before, and the reefs were accompanied by a new detail in the rigging, namely, the footrope. This ran along and below the yard and was used by the sailor to stand on when he was aloft.

Åke Classon Rålamb (1651-1718), a Swedish officer and author, published a book about shipbuilding in 1691 that has a drawing of a ship with fifty guns. This is reproduced in Figure 14, and the ship can be regarded as a Swedish design, modern in 1691. If we look at the hull, we see that the decks are almost horizontal and are parallel with the waterline, resulting in the gunports, cut through the wales. The head is much shorter than before and has a lion figurehead, while the afterbody is lower and the sheer, or the curvature of the deck, straighter and more horizontal than in older ships. The

rigging has not changed much from that of the vessel illustrated in Figure 11. The braces run as before, but the lifts of the lower yards have been moved up to the caps above the tops. The ship carries a spritsail topsail and a mizzen topsail as well as a topgallant sail at the fore- and mainmasts. The mizzen still has a bonnet (at that time, these were becoming obsolete), while the topsails, foresail, and mainsail have now a single reef each. Outside the starboard side of the main topsail, a new sail is set on a spar that has been rigged out on the main yard. The new sail was called a "studding sail," pronounced "stnn's'l." This sail did not appear very often during the latter part of the seventeenth century, but its use became more and more common during the eighteenth century and reached its peak toward the middle of the nineteenth century. After that date it became less common, and by the beginning of the twentieth century it had entirely disappeared.

In Figure 14 the tops are still circular but not entirely flat. Their leading edge carries a large crowfoot down toward the stay. Its purpose was to prevent the rim of the top from wearing a hole in the sail and also to prevent the sail from blowing in under the top when it was being furled. The reproduction of the ship is incomplete, as it does not show the staysails; but Rålamb says in the text of his book that there were four staysails, those that have been mentioned above.

It was far from easy to set the fore-topmast staysail in the midst of the complicated rig of the spritsail topmast. As a result, the latter soon disappeared. At the same time, the ship received a new spar, the jibboom, which was rigged as an extension of the bowsprit. With this followed a new staysail, the jib, which was set outside the fore-topmast staysail.

These staysails had a lifting effect on the bowsprit, quite different from the downward pull of the old spritsail, and a new stay, the bobstay, was added below the bowsprit in order to hold it down. The first known report of a bobstay is from a French source dated 1691, but it did not come into general use until a couple of decades later.

The above details were what mainly distinguished the ships of the eighteenth century from earlier ones. Figure 15 shows a large mid-eighteenth-century man-of-war. The decks are almost horizontal and are parallel with the waterline, and the rail has less sheer than older types of vessels. The bow is short and has a lion as a figurehead; the quarter galleries form an integral part of the afterbody.

It is a more functional rig. The yards have become longer, the sails are wider, and the upper sails are larger in relation to the lower sails. The after edges of the tops are now straight, which is evident from the fact that the topmast shrouds reach right out to the after edge of the tops. The bowsprit has a jibboom but still retains a rudi-

ment of the spritsail topmast, now in the form of a jack staff. All yards have footropes, and most of the sails have been provided with reefs, one in the courses and the mizzen, three in the fore- and main topsails, and two in the mizzen topsail. The spritsail also has reefs, which are placed crosswise. When the spritsail was reefed, the weather reef was taken in so that the sail became three-cornered, somewhat like the lateen mizzen, and the sail could thus be set by the wind. The function of the round hole in the spritsail was to let out the water that might wash into the concave clew of the sail. Below the jibboom we find the old spritsail topsail. It is shown in the drawing in plain view, but in reality it was sheeted to the spritsail yard, as a topsail was to the lower yard.

In addition to the fore-topmast staysail and the jib, the ship has a main-topmast staysail, a small main-topgallant staysail, and a mizzen staysail. The running gear has not changed much, but it will be noted that the head braces are moving away from the stays toward the mainmast. This change was made in order to give more space to the middle staysails and to provide stronger holds for the braces, and it was completed by about 1770.

The man-of-war represented here is the Swedish ship GÖTA LEJON, seventy-two guns, which was built in 1746 at Karlskrona. A fine ship from every point of view, when she was forty-four years old she took part in the Swedish war with Russia. She was not scrapped until 1816, when she was seventy years old.

MACEIE

15

MAC.IE

16

In 1768 the Swedish shipbuilder Fredrik Henrik af Chapman published a comprehensive book about shipbuilding called ARCHITECTURA NAVALIS MERCATORIA. Figure 16, taken from this work, shows a Swedish merchant frigate. This ship was armed in order to be able to defend herself on long voyages. She was not as large as an East Indiaman and may have been suitable for Mediterranean trade. She is shown rigged with two topgallant sails, mizzen topsail, fore-topmast staysail, and jib. The mizzen has become a gaff-rigged sail. Even in full-rigged ships, the mizzen was usually fore-and-aft rigged, as mentioned before, as an aid to the helm. As depicted, she does not carry a spritsail and carries no staysails between the masts. On the whole, her running gear is like that of the ship of the line GÖTA LEJON, but somewhat simpler. We note that the head braces lead to the mainmast. Because the foremast is stepped far ahead, the foretack leads to a small spar, called a "bumpkin," which juts out over the bow. The courses are clewed up in the clew garnets, with tacks and sheets hanging.

Among the small ships of the eighteenth century is the hooker reproduced by Chapman in the above-mentioned work. The different names for ships always seem confusing. During the early Middle Ages, when the simple rig was identical in all ships, they were named according to the different shapes of the hull. Much later, even up to the present century, when shipbuilding was highly standardized, almost all sailing ships were named according to their rig. During the eighteenth century, the custom varied—some ships were named after their rig, others according to the shape of the hull, and now and again a ship was named according to both the rig and the hull. Words like *brig, brigantine, hooker, hermaphrodite brig, ketch, schooner, sloop,* and *snow* are names that refer to the rig and are really abbreviations for "brig-rigged," "bark-rigged," "ship-rigged," and so forth. *Cat, flyboat, galley, hoy, pink,* and *xebec* refer to the hull, while words like *frigate, bark,* and *cutter* refer to the hull as well as to the rig. One can, for instance, say that a ship was built as a frigate or rigged as a frigate, that a vessel was built as a bark or rigged as a bark.

From this it is clear that the name "hooker" referred to the rig. It can be compared with a small ship rig without a foremast (Figure 17a). The square-rigged mainmast was stepped amidships, and abaft the mainmast was the mizzenmast with the mizzen and the square topsail. In order to balance all these after sails, the hooker carried a long jibboom with large headsails, forestaysail, jib, and flying jib. Abaft the mainmast, a fore-and-aft mainsail, called a "spencer," was set. Where practicable, the rig was similar to that of the larger ships; the hooker, however, often had her topmast stepped abaft the lower masthead, as shown in the picture. The lighter sails had single lifts and braces, and the large jib had a brail, which, when the sail was taken in, could pull it together and prevent it from falling into the water.

Figure 17b shows a smaller hooker. It has no mizzen topsail, and the rig is still more simplified. Among other things, the topgallant sail has no braces and was set

"flying," as the nautical term goes. The mizzen has a boom that extends beyond the stern of the ship. This is the first ship in our series that has such a mizzen boom. The mizzen boom began to come into wider use during the latter part of the eighteenth century, though it had appeared earlier in small ships. This extension of the boom over the stern also resulted in a change of name for the mizzen; from then on, it was called a "driver."

The origin of the lateen sail is unknown; it could have been developed on the Nile with the earliest of ships, from Arab shipping on the Indian Ocean, or among the islands of the Pacific.

With the penetration of the Arabs toward the West during the seventh and eighth centuries, use of the lateen sail spread to the Mediterranean area. Since the early Middle Ages, it has been the most important sail in that area for coasters and fishing boats, as well as for the oared pirate vessels of the Barbary States.

Among the latter ships were the galleys. Slender vessels with open decks and fitted with oars, the galleys were designed to attack head on, with their guns trained forward. Xebecs were somewhat larger and broader, built more for sailing, and had bulwarks to protect the personnel on deck. The guns were then placed broadside on the main deck, and the triangular lateen sail was rigged a little differently. As a rule, it was carried on the lee side, outside the shrouds; for this reason, all the shrouds were set up with tackles that could be let go, so that the lee-side shrouds would not be in the way of the yard. Figure 18 shows an eighteenth-century Algerian xebec. It carried sixteen guns on deck, trained through portholes in the bulwark, and had benches for rowers between the gun carriages. Belowdecks aft was a cabin, and above it on deck, a tent with an awning (not shown in the picture). European shipping suffered severely from the piracy of the Barbary States, and it was not until U.S. Marine action at Tripoli and the French conquest of Algiers in 1830 that piracy came to an end in the Mediterranean.

17.b

17.a

MACFIE

18.

MACBIE

19

20

Sail on the Aegean Sea: a Turkish caïque and a Greek fishing vessel from Mykonos

Swedish krejare, circa 1760

The Mediterranean, with its old culture, had many unique types of ships. Figure 19 shows a Turkish caïque, a small cargo vessel that was common at one time on the Sea of Marmara and in the eastern part of the Aegean. There were several different types, the word "caïque" being a collective word for "barge," as are the Finnish *Haxe* and the Russian *Lodja*. The particular caïque pictured is double-ended; the rudder is hanging on the sternpost abaft everything; she has a good deal of sheer and a canvas bulwark amidships.

The rig is of great interest. The mainsail is something between a Marconi main and a fore-and-aft spritsail. "Marconi sail" is the name given to the modern development of the now familiar triangular mainsail; it is also called a "jib-topped sail." This mainsail is set on an inclined spar abaft the mast and sheeted to an outrigger over the stern. The mast carries two square sails, foresail and topsail, the latter boasting another innovation, a sewn-in batten for reefing up forward; a jib is carried, and beyond this is a new sail, the flying jib. This rig might be regarded as a brigantine in that the foremast is square-rigged and the main is fore and aft.

Astern of the caïque sails a little fishing boat from Mykonos, an island north of Naxos. This craft is undecked and double-ended, and the interesting lateen sail is cut in two. The after and larger piece is laced to the mast like a gaff-rigged main, and on the forward end of the yard appears the remaining small piece, serving as a sort of staysail; it could be carried only with the wind astern, however. This lateen yard never had to be shifted to the lee side of the mast when going about. Forward, the boat carries a jib. Her sails are tanned.

Figure 20 shows another small type of eighteenth-century ship, a *krejare*. The name refers to the rig. Masts in one piece (called "pole masts") were the characteristic feature, and all yards could thus be lowered down to the deck. The rig was also known as "polacca" or "polacre." The clew lines of the topsails served as downhauls, and when the sails were taken in, the upper yards were hauled close down to the lower. When the topsails were being furled, the sailors stood on the footrope of the lower yard. The *krejare* had a driver mizzen, and her rig was an early example of the later "bark rig,"—three masts with square sails on the two forward masts.

During the Renaissance, the Portuguese and Spaniards made heroic efforts to reach the East Indies, where fabulous riches in the form of gold and spice were thought to be ready for the taking. The Portuguese sailed east around Africa, while the Spaniards, looking for a shorter route, turned westward across the Atlantic. Because the long ocean voyages were expensive enterprises that could not be undertaken by private individuals, merchants formed large trading companies that were then given trade monopolies by their governments. The Portuguese company was established as early as 1502, a few years after Vasco da Gama had returned from his first voyage; and for one hundred years thereafter, operating from their base of Goa, on the Malabar Coast, the Portuguese were the only people who traded with India. The outward- and homeward-bound ships always called at ports in Southeast Africa to get supplies of water, wood, and provisions, and to this day, these ports are called Algoa (to Goa) and Delagoa (from Goa).

The English East India Company was established in 1600, the Dutch in 1602. During the seventeenth century, the latter became the largest business enterprise of its kind, and Amsterdam the commercial center of the world. The Swedish East India Company was established in 1731 and was dissolved in 1813. The Swedish company's first ship was named FREDERICUS REX SUECIAE and sailed for Canton in 1732. In all, the company owned thirty-eight ships, which made about 130 voyages to the Far East. Of the total number of ships belonging to the company, twenty-six were built in Stockholm, while two of the others were built at Göteborg. The first of these two ships was called GÖTHEBORG and was launched on October 20, 1786. She could carry 530 lasts, or loads, one last being equal to 2.5 tons deadweight. The GÖTHEBORG was the largest ship built for the Swedish East India Company up to that time.

The East Indiamen were the largest and best-equipped merchant ships of their time and were very much like men-of-war. Figure 21 shows the GÖTHEBORG, an East Indiaman. The hull is similar to that of a naval frigate, though the latter always had finer lines. The frigate was a three-masted vessel, ship-rigged, but smaller, faster, and less heavily armed than a ship of the line. To the merchant ships, cargo space was the prime consideration; in the men-of-war, speed was more important.

The GÖTHEBORG was built with a gun deck armed with a large number of guns. She had a raised poop and a large, broad stern boasting two rows of cabin windows, together with galleries on the quarters. She was ship-rigged, and a new sail—the royal—had been added above the topgallant, so that there were four yards on every mast. Headsails had become larger and more important, the fore-staysail, jib, and flying jib nearly equal in size. The flying jib was always set on a stay from the topgallant masthead on a square-rigged foremast.

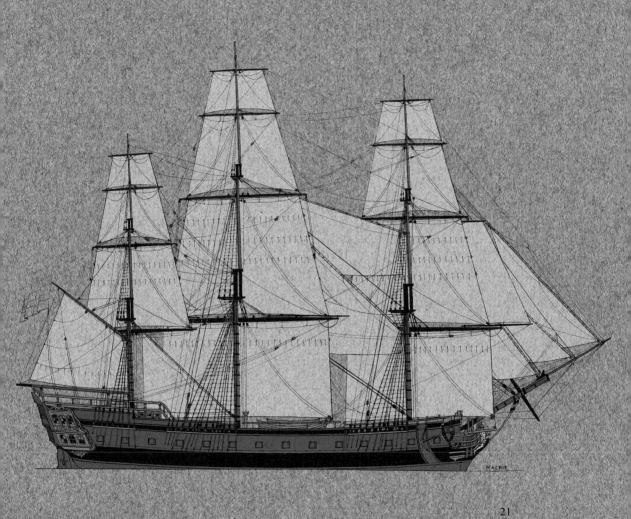

MACFIE

21

MACFIE

22

When the various staysails appeared, the spritsail lost its importance. It had always been a difficult sail to handle and had impaired visibility ahead, and it went into gradual disuse. However, the spritsail yard was still being used to support the jibboom downward, and therefore it was set with the weather yardarm aslant downward so that the jibboom guys counteracted the upward-leeward pull of the jibs. Between the masts, the ships now had a main-topmast staysail and a middle staysail, both having trapezoidal form. Outboard of the fore-topsail, the ships carried a studding sail hoisted under the topsail yardarm and hauled out to a boom on the foreyard. The main yard was similarly provided for. Later in the nineteenth century, the number of studding sails increased, and booms were rigged on several different yards.

While East Indiamen were the largest and finest merchant ships of their time, there were relatively few of them. Ordinary merchant ships were much smaller. Sloops, ketches, and schooners were the types used in home waters, while the larger ships—brigantines, brigs, and barks—sailed in the European trade.

Figure 22 shows a Swedish brig, the type that was called a "snow" during the eighteenth century. This vessel was built in 1783 at Kalmar and was named GUSTAF ADOLPH. She was of a burden of 85 lasts, nearly equal to 210 tons deadweight.

The figure shows a plain merchant vessel with a straight stem, full lines, and no figurehead. The cabin is sunk belowdecks, with windows in the broad stern, and around the raised quarterdeck is an open rail extending only as far as the mainmast. In the waist is a detachable rail that could be removed in port to facilitate loading. On deck there are two boats, the longboat and the jolly boat, the small boat being stowed in the large one. The jolly boat was used as the captain's gig and perhaps for taking the liberty watch ashore if the ship was moored. There is an etymological connection between the terms "jolly" and "yawl." In Figure 22 the foresail and the topgallant sails hang in the clew lines, but the mainsail is not bent. The sail on the small mast abaft the mainmast is called the "trysail." It cannot be called a "driver" or "mizzen," because such a sail must be set on the mizzenmast of a ship; neither can it be called a "mainsail," because this name refers to the square sail below the main yard. The spritsail is not bent, and the spritsail yard serves mainly as a support to the jibboom.

The snow GUSTAF ADOLPH was one of the many small vessels that sailed under simple conditions and with a small crew in Northern European waters without attracting much attention. During the latter half of the eighteenth century, the bark began to appear among them, and it became more and more common in the nineteenth century. The bark had three masts and was somewhat larger than the brig. It probably developed from the snow when the trysail mast was moved away from the mainmast and provided with shrouds, for in a bark the foremast and mainmast are square-rigged, and the mizzen is fore and aft.

Figure 23 shows such a bark, the FORTUNA, of about 120 lasts, built at Umeå, North Sweden, in 1792. She is somewhat larger than the GUSTAF ADOLPH but has the the same flush deck and, instead of a bulwark, an open rail in the waist to protect the quarterdeck forward to the mainmast. The two boats are stowed amidships on deck; the foremast is stepped far forward, and aft of it can be seen the windlass with its horizontal barrel.

FORTUNA was also a plain vessel and was rigged without royals, but she had several four-cornered staysails. Those in front of the mainmast were the main staysail, the main-topmast staysail, and the middle staysail, and set on the mizzen stay was the mizzen staysail. The tack of the mainsail was clewed up and the tack of the driver hauled up to let the wind into the mainsail and thereby make it draw better. When the FORTUNA also had her studding sails set, the tack of the square lower studding sail was hauled out to windward to the lower studding-sail boom rigged from the fore channel. The spritsail yard had no sail and served mainly to spread the jibboom guys, as in the snow GUSTAF ADOLPH.

By 1800, the spritsail yard was disappearing, to be replaced by two short spars, or struts, that started downward and outboard from the bowsprit. Their purpose was to eliminate the necessity for having to haul around the spritsail yard every time the ship went about. FORTUNA was fitted out this way.

Soon these two spars evolved into one central spar, the martingale boom, or dolphin striker, placed at the cap of the bowsprit. Martingale stays from the jibboom and martingale guys to the bows effectively held the jibboom down against the upward pull of the jibs.

During the Napoleonic Wars, it became the custom to paint the men-of-war black with horizontal yellow bands around the black-painted gunports, replacing the earlier tar and yellow-brown colors. The bands were soon being painted white. This style was begun in the English Navy and used to be called "painted Nelson-fashion." It is now usually called "painted ports." The custom spread quickly to merchant ships that had neither guns nor portholes belowdecks. This was done not only for decorative reasons; it was also a form of camouflage, since an enemy—for example, a pirate—could not at a distance discern whether there were really guns behind the black "gunports." Painted ports, however, outlived the purpose of camouflage, and no one confused the last of these sailing ships with men-of-war. (See Figures 29, 41, and 57.)

During the latter part of the eighteenth century, the bottoms of men-of-war were sheathed in copper in order to protect them against teredo worms. This required that the bolts in the bottom of the ships also be made of copper, to prevent electrolytic action between two different metals in salt water. This soon became general practice among merchant ships that made voyages in tropical waters.

Early in the nineteenth century, large ships looked quite different from their predecessors of 1790. The profile was straighter, with little sheer, and the hull was painted black or black and white. Each mast had four yards, sometimes five, and the ships carried many staysails and had a jibboom with a martingale boom.

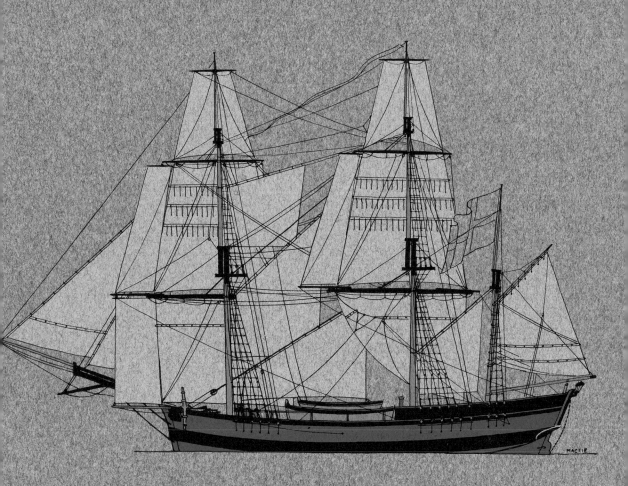

MACFIE

23

24

The brigantine BULL, *from Stockholm, built in 1841, the second Swedish ship to sail around the world*

Figure 24 shows the BULL, a small brigantine-rigged ship built in 1841. The hull has little sheer and is painted black with a white band and has black-painted ports. Even the boats are painted black. One is hanging in davits on the starboard quarter, which ships of the eighteenth century did not have. The yellow metal sheathing shows along the waterline. The rig is typical of the middle of the nineteenth century, when the brigantine was very similar to the brig but had a simplified rig on the mainmast. The foremast, on the other hand, has the usual square rig with foresail, topsail, topgallant sail, and royal, but with a trysail bent to a trysail mast abaft the foremast. Because the mainstay was set up at the deck, the trysail could not have a boom, and when going about, its foot had to be lifted over the stay. The mainmast has a lower mast and a topmast, a large fore-and-aft mainsail, a square topsail, and a topgallant sail on the topmast. The vessel has three headsails, namely, the fore-topmast staysail, which is furled in the repro-

duction, a jib, and a flying jib. Below the bowsprit is the martingale boom mentioned above. In addition, there are three studding sails, known as the lower, topmast, and topgallant studding sails.

As ships grew in size, the large topsails became increasingly difficult to handle. When the area of the sail had to be reduced in a storm, the reefing was an especially hard job that required a large crew. In 1841 the American sea captain R. B. Forbes devised a method of dividing the topsail in two by putting a new yard in the rig for the lower half of the sail. The first vessel thus rigged was the American topsail schooner MIDAS. Another American sea captain, Frederic Howes, improved on the Forbes method of rigging in 1853, and the Howes rig with double-topsail yards soon became general in all large and medium-sized merchant ships. It is not known which British ship was the first to be rigged with the Howes topsails, but the first Swedish ship with these was probably the INDIAMAN, built at Gävle in 1854.

The brig rig was very popular for a long time because of its maneuverability. The advantage of a square sail is that it can be braced in such a way that its front side catches the wind, and thus the ship is taken aback. With her symmetrical rig, a brig could sail forward or backward, stand still in the water, or turn on the spot, all depending on how the sails were braced. In exotic ports where there were no towboats, the brigs could manage through their own maneuvering better than other ships. The English collier brigs that sailed from Newcastle to London managed on their own in the narrow waters of the Thames, as did the brigs that sailed in the coffee trade from Brazil, where the ports often had no towboats.

Figure 25 shows a brig rigged with double-topsail yards according to the Howes system. The lower topsail yards are trussed to the cap of the lower mast. The upper yards were hoisted and lowered like the old single-topsail yard. The rig of the lower topsail yard is similar to that of the lower yards, while the upper topsail yard has the same rig as the single-topsail yard of earlier days. Apart from the new lower topsail yard, the rig (with courses, topgallant sails, and royals) is like the older rig. The bowsprit has a martingale boom with a fully developed rig, and the flying jib is set on the fore-topgallant stay.

The main-topmast staysail is set, but the main-topgallant staysail is furled abaft the fore lower masthead. The brig's trysail has no boom, and the tack was hauled up in order to let the wind into the mainsail. The mainsail's clew was pulled up to allow the staysail and forecourse to fill. The brig is equipped with a whole set of studding sails, but in the drawing the fore lower studding sail and the fore-topgallant studding sail are not set.

The hull has a moderate sheer, and there are a deckhouse and a cabin on deck. The longboat stands in chocks over the main hatch forward of the mainmast. The yellow metal sheathing shows that she was built for long voyages in the tropics. Let us imagine that she is coming from Brazil, bound for Antwerp with coffee. The voyage is almost over, and outside Vlissingen she meets the Dutch pilot cutter and takes a pilot aboard. Being a smart brig, she sails up the Schelde River right to the dock gates of Antwerp. The brig shown is the DAHLKARLSÅ, built at Dahlkarlså, North Sweden, in 1862. The DAHLKARLSÅ was of 300 net register tons and carried about 440 tons deadweight.

Early in the nineteenth century, with growing industrialization, it became increasingly important that sea voyages be shortened. Fast sailing ships existed, such as small ships built as privateers and blockade runners in time of war. There were also smugglers and slave ships in times of war and peace for whom speed in pursuit or escape was a necessity.

MACFIE

26

After the American Revolutionary War, and more so after the war with England of 1812-1815, American shipbuilders, who were not bound by tradition, began to build faster vessels, schooners and brigs that were employed in the most profitable trades in the world. These vessels were mainly built in Virginia and Maryland, where the area around Chesapeake Bay had long been a center for the shipbuilding industry. These small fast craft were known throughout the world as Baltimore clippers.

Figure 26 shows a Baltimore clipper built about 1820; it is rigged as a two-topsail schooner, both masts having fore-and-aft sails, with the mainmast aft. The hull is long, low, and broad. She was built with a greater draft aft and a raked stem that produced an overhanging bow. This was the so-called clipper bow, which provided a sharp entry into the water. The lightening of the hull, with the consequent reduction of "wetted" area, accounted for much of her speed. The development of "faster" hulls proceeded along these lines, and the underwater profile was diminished from the bow aft and the stern forward. Sharper bottoms were designed, as well as bows with steeply rising sides or, finally, in Donald McKay's clipper ships, hollow bows. The masts of this clipper were high and raked and carried huge fore-and-aft sails. As the mainstay was set up at the deck, the gaff-foresail could not have a boom, and every time the vessel went about, the sail had to be brailed in to the mast and carried over the stay to the new lee side. In addition to the new fore-and-aft sails, the schooner carried a square topsail and topgallant sail on both masts. She was armed with eight small guns on the open deck, which had only hatches and skylights to the accommodations below.

The names of the different types of schooners vary to such an extent that no one really knows what they ought to be called. The Baltimore clipper in Figure 26, which has a square sail on each mast, with both masts rigged schooner-fashion, was usually called a "two-topsail schooner," while the BULL in Figure 24, with a complete-ly square-rigged foremast, was known as a "brigantine." Schooners with a square topsail on only the foremast were called "topsail schooners," and the type that was entirely without square sails was called a "fore-and-aft schooner." The ship that had a square-rigged foremast and a fore-and-aft mainmast with fore-and-aft topsail was called a "hermaphrodite brig." The brigantine differs in that the mainmast had a fore-and-aft mainsail but square topsails.

In the 1800's the coastal population in New England carried on whaling with small vessels in coastal waters, and at the beginning of the eighteenth century they began to hunt spermaceti whales in the Atlantic. The oil of the spermaceti whale was of a much higher quality than that which had been extracted earlier; in time, hunting spermaceti whales became the most lucrative aspect of whaling. Other nations were also engaged in whaling, but the Americans from Massachusetts were still in the lead, with New Bedford and Nantucket as their chief ports. In 1815, after the war with England, American whalers sailed on all seas, the Indian Ocean and the Pacific as well as the Atlantic.

At that time the leviathan was hunted in oar-propelled whaleboats from which harpoons were flung. Spermaceti, cachalot, and Greenland whales were sought, for these types swim slowly and float when killed. Because dorsal-finned whales, especially the large blue whale of the Antarctic, swim faster and sink when they are killed, they can be hunted successfully only by modern methods. Whaling of the old days cannot be compared with the mechanized extermination of today, when whales are hunted by helicopter and submarine radar and are killed with harpoon guns and explosive shells.

Before the Norwegian Svend Foyn invented the grenade harpoon in 1864, whaling was a thrilling and dangerous occupation. It was then necessary to come so close to the animal in a whaleboat that it could be reached with a harpoon thrown by hand; the whale was then killed with a long lance.

27. *American whaling bark from the 1850's, hunting for spermaceti whal*

28. *The American clipper* FLYING CLOUD, *1851, which holds the record of twice sailing from New York*
San Francisco in 89 da

Figure 27 shows an American whaler, circa 1850. She is bark-rigged and lies in a calm, bright, sunny tropical sea. The lower sails are furled to keep them out of the way because the blubber tryworks are in use, and her topgallant sails hang in the clew lines. She has the topsails and fore-and-aft sails set, but the royal yards are rigged down. The sail set abaft the mizzenmast, formerly called the "driver," was by this time being called the "spanker." The whaleboats are hoisted under fixed oak davits, ready to be lowered when required.

The early nineteenth century saw more fast sailing ships being built. They differed from older ships by being longer, by having less draft in relation to their beam, and by having long, narrow bows with concave waterlines forward. In the last, they also differed from the early Baltimore schooners, and the concave bow was regarded as the most important characteristic of the clippers. Such clippers were constructed early in the century at Aberdeen, where a schooner, the SCOTTISH MAID, was built as early as 1839. But in building full-rigged ships, America was ahead, and the RAINBOW, constructed in New York in 1845, is considered by American authorities to be the first clipper in the world.

Figure 28 shows one of these American clippers, the FLYING CLOUD, of 1,783 net register tons, built at Boston in 1851 by Donald McKay. She was 232 feet long overall; she had a beam of 41 feet and a hold depth of 21 feet. She was the only sailing ship in the world that twice sailed from New York to San Francisco around Cape Horn in less than 90 days. On her first voyage, in 1851, she made the trip in 89 days and 21 hours; and on her fourth voyage, in 1854, it took her only 89 days and 8 hours. She was rigged with single topsails, each with four reefs, topgallant sails with one reef, royals, and skysails. She naturally carried staysails on most of the stays and had a whole set of studding sails, including the royals; she had studding-sail booms on the topgallant

yards and had jewel blocks for the royal studding sails on the royal yardarms.

The standing rigging was of Russian hemp, which the American shipbuilders imported from Riga. The rig was modern, according to American advanced methods, with forged so-called patent trusses for the lower yards and chains for the halyards and sheets of the square sails. Her long, sheathed black-painted hull was so different from that of the Swedish East Indiaman shown in Figure 21, for example, that she represented a new age. The smooth side of the ship was decorated with a white figurehead, and there was a carved ornament around the elliptical stern. On deck there was a raised forecastlehead forward, a deckhouse abaft the foremast, and a large cabin aft. Right aft she had a short quarterdeck, the rail of which is seen abaft the mizzen rigging in the illustration. She had two boats on top of the deckhouse and four more boats on skids abaft the main rigging.

The drawing shows the FLYING CLOUD from the lee side. She has three headsails, namely, fore-topmast staysail and inner and outer jib. Here the foremast staysail is not a flying jib, because this would be set on the fore-topgallant stay, as mentioned before. The lee side of the square sails shows the buntlines and leech ropes that, together with the clew lines, served to furl the sails. A distinction is made between the buntlines, which are attached to the foot of the sail, and the leech ropes, which are attached to the leeches. The courses have four of the former and two of the latter, while the topsails and topgallant sails have two of each. The royals have only one buntline with a crowfoot, while the skysails have no buntlines at all. These sails were fairly small and were furled before the wind became too strong. In order to be able to sail closer by the wind, the FLYING CLOUD was rigged with bowlines right up to the topgallant sails, which was an unusual arrangement for merchant ships of this period.

27

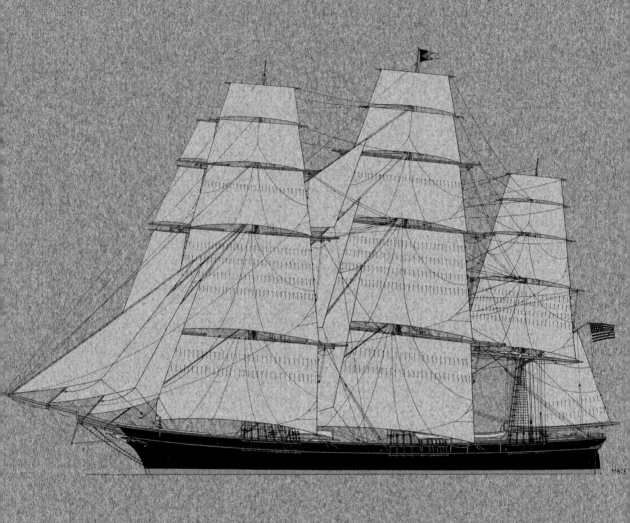

29

MACFIE

30

Trade with India was an important branch of England's worldwide shipping. It had its roots in the East India Company of the eighteenth century, was always carried on from London, and survived to a certain extent in its old form in regard to both organization and ships. The latter developed into a characteristically somewhat old-fashioned type, often built at the yards at Blackwall, which made them rather similar to naval frigates, and they were universally known as "Blackwall frigates." They were the East Indiamen of the nineteenth century. They sailed regularly to Calcutta, but at the beginning of the Australian gold rush, they began to sail to Melbourne and Sydney.

Figure 29 shows such a Blackwall frigate, LA HOGUE, built in 1855 at Sunderland for Duncan Dunbars Shipping Company in London. She was of 1,330 net register tons, with the dimensions 226 by 35 feet, and she sadly ended her days as a coal hulk at Madeira and was broken up in 1897. The picture shows a full-rigged vessel; it has painted ports, a large figurehead, a somewhat heavy stern with small galleries on the quarters, and large external channels for the rigging. The ship has a large forecastlehead, a long poop with several cabins for passengers, four boats under davits, and two boats housed on the top of the deckhouse. The boats are painted black with white bottoms, which was the fashion in English ships during the 1860's. The rig is strong, with shrouds of wire, and is equipped with the Howes double topsails, with clew lines on the upper topsails as well as the lower; she has four headsails, namely, fore-topmast staysail, inner and outer jib, and flying jib.

The ship had no crossjack (pronounced "crojack"), or mizzen course, bent, as it could not be set properly in the small space between the mainmast and the mizzenmast, where the lifeboats were carried. Instead, she carried a large driver, or spanker, and a mizzen staysail as well as a mizzen-topmast staysail. The name "spanker" was substituted for "driver" from about the middle of the nineteenth century. In the picture, only a fore-top-mast studding sail is set, but as a rule these early ships carried a whole set of studding sails.

The large ships mentioned above, aristocrats of the sea, were used for trading voyages to California, India, and Australia. In addition, there were many small vessels in coastal trade that were often well built, fast sailing, and well cared for by their crews. Their seamanship was very different from that of the large sailing ships. The latter liked the open sea best, with anchors lashed down on the forecastlehead, the cables unshackled and stowed below, and the hawsepipes stoppered to keep a dry deck under the forecastlehead; while the coastal sailers learned to navigate in narrow waters with anchors ready.

Figure 30 shows a small topgallant-rigged schooner, usually called a "topsail schooner," although that name really refers to a rig with topsails only. This vessel was built of oak in Schleswig in 1850 and was called HANSINE. She was acquired by Simrishamn, Sweden, in 1896, when she was renamed HANSINA. She changed her home port several times and was scrapped in the early 1930's, when she was more than eighty years old.

In the picture, she is seen from the lee side under full sail. She has four headsails. Here we lose the set order that was characteristic of the headsails in a square-rigged ship, that is, the forestaysail, inner jib, outer jib, and flying jib. What is illogical is that the jibs are carried on stays from the lower masthead. The sails abaft each mast under the gaffs are the foresail and mainsail, the latter with a gaff-topsail above. The square sails are the topsail and topgallant sail. The latter is bent to its yard without the wooden rod or wire rope called the "jack-stay," to which the sails were more usually secured, but is fastened directly to the yard. The vessel has only one deckhouse, where the small crew lived, the men at the forward end of the house and the officers aft. Abaft the steering wheel is a small house with two small compartments, the lamp locker on the one side and a lavatory on the other. The only boat of the vessel is hanging in fixed davits fitted athwartships over the stern.

In a schooner the aftermast is the largest, and the masts are called "foremast" and "mainmast." In a ketch the forward mast is the largest, and the masts are called "mainmast" and "mizzenmast." Figure 31 shows such a ketch, common in Northern European coastal waters. In the reproduction, she has a vertical spar fitted on the foreside of the mainmast and carrying two square sails, a forecourse, and a topsail. In addition, she carries four staysails, namely, the forestaysail (not set in the picture), inner jib, outer jib, and flying jib. She also carries a mainsail with a main topsail above and a spanker with a mizzen topsail.

Both the gaff-topsails are four-cornered and bent to short yards. In effect, this provided a fore-and-aft sail that was square-rigged at the head and particularly use-ful in light winds. The boom topping lifts were served over (wound around) at intervals with bits of unraveled rope braided together to prevent the lifts from chafing the sails. The term for this antichafing gear is "baggy-wrinkles."

On deck the vessel has a small galley abaft the main-mast and a cabin farther aft, the top of which extends over the steering position. The helmsman stood on a grating so that his head reached up through a round hole in the top of the house. This arrangement protected the helmsman and was fairly common on small vessels on the Baltic. The drawing is of a ketch called EXPERIMENT, built in 1857 near Kalmar, Sweden. She sailed in the Baltic trade until 1930, when she was broken up after more than seventy years of service.

In addition to the large deepwater ships and the small coastal vessels, there were a large number of medium-sized ships engaged in more extensive coastal shipping and shorter ocean voyages. Among sailing ships of from 500 to 1,000 register tons, the bark was the most important. They were more popular than full-rigged ships of this size and could be handled by a smaller crew.

The sailing capacity of a ship depends on many factors, such as the shape of the hull below water, the draft, stiffness, trim, and the degree of cleanliness of the bottom. If all these factors are assumed to have been alike and if the sails on the foremast and mainmast also are assumed to have been alike, then the bark did not sail so well as the ship in moderate weather with the wind on the beam. When the two ran before the wind, the height of the rigging and the width of the sails decided the sail area, and both sailed alike. In a strong wind, when sails were shortened, they were equally good. When they sailed by the wind in rough weather, the fact that the rigging of the bark caught less wind constituted a real advantage. The few advantages of the full-rigged ship, therefore, did not outbalance its disadvantages, and among medium-sized vessels the bark was much more common than the ship.

Figure 32 shows such a small bark sailing under the French flag. Her name was PERSISTANT, and she was built in 1865 in Nantes for shipowners in Le Havre, to which port she belonged until 1893, when she was taken off the register. She was of 445 net register tons, with registered dimensions of 145 by 30 feet. The picture shows a wooden ship painted white with a small forecastlehead, a deckhouse, and a low poop, called a "monkey poop," on both sides of the cabin. Athwartships, on the top of the deckhouse, lies a small skiff, while the lifeboats lie upside down on skids inside the main rigging. There are downhauls to the upper topsail yards and lifts on the lower. Above the topsails, she carries topgallant sails and royals, and all the sails, with the exception of the upper topsails, are clewed up to the bunt.

The vessel has a standing gaff, and the spanker is furled—brailed in to the mast. She has four headsails. The reefs in the courses and the upper topsails had no reef points, but reef lines stretched across the sails from leech to leech. In addition, the yards were equipped with several short gaskets with which the reef line was tied to the yard when the reef was taken in. This reefing method, called "French reefing," differed from the usual one, where the reef points in the sail were tied around the yard.

When the British Navigation Laws were repealed in 1849, English shipbuilders became more exposed to foreign, mainly American, competition. Through the Merchant Shipping Act of 1854, they were also released from old rules of ship measurements that had favored ships that were too narrow and had too much depth to sail well. In the late 1840's, American clippers sailed with cargoes of tea from China to London faster than had been possible earlier. In fact, it can be legitimately claimed that America, not Britannia, ruled the waves in the middle decades of the 19th century. In number of ships, in total deadweight, and in sheer sailing exploits, the American vessels and their mariners must be accredited primacy. An American vessel, the clipper SOVEREIGN OF THE SEAS, sailed faster, at 22 knots, than any other sailing ship before or since, running from New York to Liverpool in 13 days and 14 hours. More significantly, the British armed forces chartered American bottoms to transport their troops both to the Crimea in 1855 and to the Sepoy Mutiny in 1857. Industrial development made speedier voyages desirable, and at an even earlier date the Scots had built fast schooners.

The outcome of this was that the English shipyards began to build fast sailing ships generally, and in a few years the English China clipper, the tea clipper, was created, which many regarded as the finest sailing vessel in the world. It is prudent to mention here that a ship can be appraised from many different points of view. Some advocated the American clippers; others, the beautiful English iron clippers in the Australian trade in the 1870's; while the large, mainly German, steel sailing ships of later days also had their admirers.

The English China clipper, however, ranks very high on the scale. The tea trade was centralized in London at an early date. During the latter part of the 1840's, American ships dominated the tea trade, but after 1850 the English soon obtained sole control. The exclusive tea-clipper trade was, however, of short duration, and it decreased quickly after the opening of the Suez Canal in 1869, when the finest sailing ships turned to other routes.

The China clippers were generally of 700 to 900 register tons, with fine lines, and initially were built of first-class oak or teak, but after 1863 they were of composite construction, with frames and beams of iron but with planking of wood. They had a large sail plan and were kept like luxury yachts and sailed with great skill. One of the last, the CUTTY SARK, built in 1869, still exists; it now lies as a museum ship in dry dock near the National Maritime Museum at Greenwich.

Figure 33 shows another of these beautiful clippers, the NORMAN COURT, built in 1869 in Glasgow for shipowners in London. She was of 834 net register tons, was 200 feet long overall, and had a beam of 33 feet. She sailed for some years in the China trade and thereafter made alternate voyages to Australia and China. In 1878 she was rerigged as a bark, and in 1881 she ran ashore at Holyhead and became a wreck. The picture shows a ship with fine lines, long, straight bows, a narrow stern, and an enormous spread of sail, stretching in one unbroken line from stem to stern and giving the impression of a large yacht. She has four headsails, double topsails, topgallant sails, royals, and a main skysail. All sails are clewed up to the bunt; she has two reefs in the topsails and a standing spanker gaff. On deck she has a richly paneled deckhouse with two boats stowed on top; in addition, there are two boats on skids on either side abaft the mainmast, all stowed upside down. There is a low monkey poop aft on the same level as the main rail. The cabin is situated on the main deck, and one half of its height extends above the poop.

A ship like the NORMAN COURT was an aristocrat of the sea, but when sailed she required continuous vigilance. If she had been struck by a squall with all sails set, the effect might well have been disastrous.

MACPIE

33

34

It can be said that the barkentine was next to the bark among the three-masted sailing ships, not counting full-rigged ships. She was also one of the last sailing vessels developed as an international type, with square-rigged foremast and fore-and-aft-rigged main and mizzen.

At the beginning of the nineteenth century, this rig was to be found occasionally in three-masted steamships, all of which had sails, and it was only toward the middle of that century that the rig became more common, mainly in America. Like the brigantine, the barkentine passed through several stages of development, with a different number of square sails placed on the foremast and the mainmast. She was also known under various names, such as "schooner bark" and "jackass bark." Sailing ships of this size were generally constructed of wood, but there were also barkentines built of steel, and these were generally made in England.

Figure 34 shows a Swedish barkentine, the FLORIDA, built in 1874. The FLORIDA was of 312 gross tons and of 298 net register tons; she was 110 feet long, with a beam of 24 feet. Her bottom was metal sheathed, and for many years she was engaged in Atlantic voyages, mostly on the West Indian and Brazilian routes. In 1893 she was resheathed for the last time, and toward the end of the century she was regarded as too small for long voyages and was mainly engaged in the North Sea trade. On a voyage in 1910, the FLORIDA ran ashore during a storm and fog and became a total loss.

The picture shows her under full sail as seen from the starboard-windward side. The deckhouse is built around the foremast, the boats are stowed one in the other on the main hatch, and the cabin aft is surrounded by a low poop. The double topsail now has its final shape, with downhauls to the upper topsail yard. Three of the staysails between the masts are four-cornered, while the main staysail has a boom to spread its foot and a topping lift leading to the mainmast. It was common practice to have the main boom's topping lift also lead to the mast behind so as not to chafe on the sail. The stays of the mizzenmast led from the main-topmast head in order to ease the work on the main topsail when going about, and both the gaffs had vangs to steady them.

Earlier, mention was made of the two-masted schooner that appeared with many different rigs and under various names. After the older types shown in Figures 24 and 26 had disappeared, the hermaphrodite brig became the most important. It was now known as a "brigantine" and was distinguished by its square-rigged foremast and fore-and-aft-rigged mainmast.

Figure 35 shows such a brigantine, JOHAN, built in 1884 at Nordmaling, North Sweden. She was made with surplus wood from three large ships built earlier at the same shipyard. The foremast is identical with that of a brig, while the mainmast carries a fore-and-aft mainsail and a gaff-topsail. Between the masts, she has four staysails—main staysail, middle staysail, main-topmast staysail, and main-topgallant staysail. The headsails are foretopmast staysail and inner and outer jib.

JOHAN was a strong, heavy schooner of 200 net register tons. When new, she was sheathed and made several long voyages. In 1898 she was sold to Skåne and a few years later was sold again. On a voyage from Sundsvall to Shoreham with a cargo of wood, she ran ashore on the Goodwin Sands in a fog on November 1, 1912. The crew was rescued by the Ramsgate lifeboat, and later JOHAN was towed into Dover, where she was condemned.

Besides the international types of sailing ships formerly found everywhere, many local types existed in certain areas. Among these, perhaps the Chinese junk is the most remarkable. The junk is not a uniform type of craft, and the name should be used collectively when describing Chinese sailing vessels. Along China's long coastline, from the Gulf of Chihli in the north to Hainan in the south, there were many types—trading junks, fishing junks, river junks, and so on. Figure 36 shows a cargo junk from Amoy. An eye was painted on each bow, to enable her to find her way across the sea. This custom is still widespread, and the eyes appear to this day on fishing boats in the Mediterranean and in the East. "Suppose no eye; no can see," the Chinese sailor says in his broken English, a perfect example of Eastern logic. The rig of a junk is, strictly speaking, a lugsail arrangement. The sail would be to the leeward of the mast on

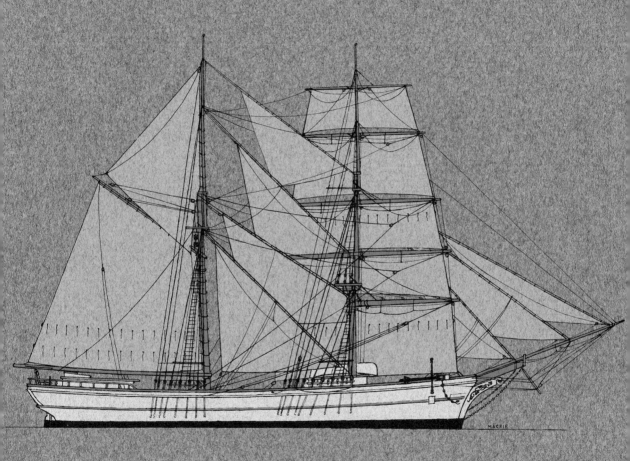

MACFIE

35

37

a starboard tack, as is pictured. The sail was not dipped when the vessel came about onto a port tack but was flattened against the windward side of the mast. This would be a standing lugsail, as differentiated from the dipping lug of the Arabian dhow's lateen sails, which were dipped on coming about in order to be kept to leeward. The sails consist of matting and are kept flat with inserted bamboo battens, which, together with the complicated sheets, allow good sailing by the wind. Many types of junks sail well, but not so the fishing junks, which often drift with trawlnets; and the flat-bottomed river junks are the worst of all.

Chinese sea trade is as ancient as its junks, which are sailed by excellent crews. Sigurd Sternvall reports heading in for the northern entrance of the Shanghai delta in a northeaster with a trading junk from Chefoo that payed out a bamboo hawser to drag astern in order to prevent the junk from broaching to. When the craft came into the breakers on the bar, the cook kept pouring bean oil on the hawser to calm the breakers. Calming sea with oil is not a Western invention after all!

Another exotic vessel is the Arabian dhow. There are several types, and, like the name "junk," the word "dhow" should be interpreted as a collective one that is used internationally. Smaller types are said to be known under so many local names that no outsider can keep track of them. The largest type, which has a richly sculptured and painted stern, like an East Indiaman of the eighteenth century, is called *baghla* or *bagala*. Other names are *bum* or *boom, ganja, zambuk,* and *zarook.* Figure 37 shows a *zambuk*. These large vessels make only one voyage a year, from the Persian Gulf to ports in East Africa. They always sail southward during the northeast monsoon and await the southwest monsoon for the return passage. On their outward passage, they carry all the products of the Arabian world, often salt and

dates, which they can sell in Zanzibar and other ports. The return cargo is usually building timber or the like, which treeless Arabia always needs. The ships never beat but run with the monsoon, according to a sailing tradition as ancient as the Arabs' business methods. When a dhow calls at some small out-of-the-way Arabian port, her rudder is taken ashore and is kept by the port authorities until the master obtains clearance outward.

The large ships are well built of Malabar teak and often have brightly painted details. The bottom is covered with a coat of unslaked lime and camel fat which protects it against borers. In Figure 37 the low side amidships has a loose bulwark made of a matting of palm fibers, and there is also an awning stretched over the poop. The long, straight stem is characteristic of this type of dhow. The sails are always set on the lee side of the shrouds, which consist of loose tackles. When going about, the yards are placed vertically along the mast, and the sails are taken around ahead to the new lee side.

During the latter half of the nineteenth century, competition from steamships arose. On long ocean voyages, the sailing ships still reigned supreme, but in European waters and on the North Atlantic, competition was already keen. When the Suez Canal was opened in 1869, this affected ships sailing from Europe to East India and China, and thereafter there were only two long routes on which the European sailing ships could hold their own, namely, to Australia and around Cape Horn to the West Coast of America.

Thus the sailing ships had few special routes, and for the most part they had to sail in the tramp trade. The Australian wool trade, however, was different, and during the period 1870-1880, it employed the finest iron clippers of that time. Every year, they raced to London, where the cargoes that arrived first fetched the best prices at the wool sales.

Growing industry created both directly and indirectly a larger demand for goods, and this led to an increase in the size of ships. The transition from wood to iron and steel also made larger ships possible. In 1860 a ship was regarded as large if she was of 1,200 register tons; in 1870, of 1,500 tons; in 1880, of up to 2,000 tons; while the largest ships in the 1890's were of more than 3,000 tons. An exception to this size rating was the American clipper ship GREAT REPUBLIC, built in 1853; she was of 4,555 tons.

Figure 38 shows an English steel sailing ship, chosen to represent several hundred similar large ships that carried on a losing battle against the increasing number of steamships during the last decades of the nineteenth century. This ship was built in 1882 by Harland & Wolff of Belfast for Ismay, Imrie & Co. of Liverpool and was launched in January and given the name GARFIELD. Of 2,347 gross and of 2,290 net register tons and with the registered dimensions of 300 by 41 by 25 feet, she was one of the largest sailing vessels of her time. In the same year, Harland & Wolff built another vessel to the same lines, which was called LORD DOWNSHIRE and was rigged with four masts. Like all the Harland & Wolff ships, the GARFIELD was well built, and she was generally regarded as a beautiful and well-kept craft.

In large, lengthy ships, the rig could not be built proportionally as high as the increased length of the hull, and in Figure 38 we see the GARFIELD with her strong but apparently low rigging. The rig is traditional, but we discover two innovations, namely, the bowsprit and the jibboom are now joined into one spar, called a "spike bowsprit," and the lower masts and topmasts are joined together, resulting in one long spar. At the time that the GARFIELD was built, this practice was just going into vogue, and it was made possible because spars were being constructed of steel instead of wood. Abaft the mainmast, we also see an unusual sail, something between a staysail and a trysail. It was a special storm sail, set only in very heavy weather.

In this more or less chronological description, we now turn to smaller vessels. Everywhere, there were small, locally built vessels that, though important in their own sphere, exerted little or no influence on the larger, oceangoing vessels.

In waters adjacent to the English Channel, mainly in Brittany but also on the south coast of England, the lugger, Figure 39, was to be found. It did carry small cargoes, but is was mostly used for fishing. These vessels also played their part in smuggling and as privateers in wartime. The French lugger was called a *chasse-marée,* a sea hunter. It is not quite clear whether the name originally referred to the shape of the hull or to the rigging, but nowadays a lugger is understood to be a vessel rigged with lugsails. It cannot be said with any certainty that this sail was developed from the Northern European square sail, which was trimmed for sailing by the wind, or from the Mediterranean lateen sail, with its front part cut off. The hull of the lugger was also characteristic, with a straight stem, a sharp bottom, and a lean, beautifully shaped counter. From the drawing, we note that she has a capstan, which was used for hauling fishing nets and lines, aft of the mainmast. The low scuttle, seen behind the capstan, was placed on the starboard side of the deck and did not prevent the capstan from revolving. The red sails generally used by fishermen in Northern and Western Europe were tanned. Formulas varied, but, generally, a concoction evolved from oak bark and water, with a little Stockholm tar or tallow, ferrous sulfate, and color, and this mixture, while still warm, was applied to the spread-out sails.

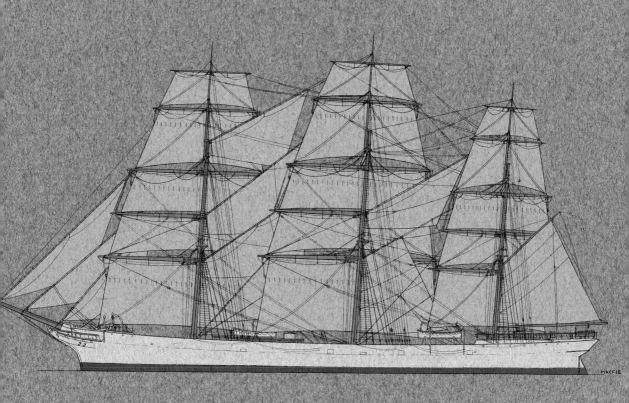

MACFIE

38

MAGEE

39

MACPIE

40

Offshore fishing is closely related to merchant shipping. European vessels that fished for cod and halibut on the Newfoundland banks sailed regularly across the Atlantic from Spain, Portugal, and France. French bank fishing was mainly carried on from the Channel ports in the Gulf of Saint-Malo. Figure 40 shows a French fishing schooner, the CHAMPENOISE, from Granville. The hull was clipper-built, and she sailed well. She has only one small deckhouse, the cook's galley, just forward of the mainmast. The galley was on deck for air and, if possible, was located at the theoretical center of motion should the vessel be pitching in heavy seas. On the top of the low cabin are several tubs containing coiled cod lines, and her boats are stacked on top of one another by the foremast. These boats are of a type that is universally known by the name "dory."

Of American origin, the dories have sloping sides, and the thwarts are detachable so that the boats can be stowed one inside or on top of the other, as shown in the drawing. They are in general use by all who fish using handlines on the Newfoundland banks.

The rigging of the CHAMPENOISE is that of an ordinary topsail schooner. One special point of interest is the square fore-topsail, which is equipped with a Colling and Pinkney roller reefing (patented in 1863). Below the topsail yard, a special spar is mounted, around which the sail is rolled. This was done by means of a chain that was rolled around the ends of the spar and worked by tackles from the deck.

As early as the fifteenth century, large ships were rigged with four masts, but they had nothing in common with the large four-masted square-rigged ships of the nineteenth century. A few of the latter were built very early in the century as an experiment, and it is reported that as early as 1801 a French privateer was built in Bordeaux that was square-rigged on four masts. In America a few large four-masters were built of wood, but it was only when England built the first four-masted iron ship, in 1875, that this rig for large ships became general. The first four-masted ships were ship-rigged, but, as in the case of the three-masted vessels, the bark proved to be a more flexible rig to handle. By the end of the century, the four-masted bark was the most economical ship.

Figure 41 shows an English four-masted full-rigged steel ship, built in 1887 by Barclay Curle at Glasgow for R. & J. Craig of that city. She was given the name the COUNTY OF LINLITHGOW and was of 2,200 gross tons.

Apart from the four masts, she has the traditional rig, with single topgallant sails and royals, and a rigged-out jibboom with four headsails. The mainmast and the mizzenmast have small trysails, which were used as storm sails when the courses were furled. The hull has beautiful but somewhat laborious port painting; she has two houses on deck and carries boats on skids forward of the mainmast and under davits by the jiggermast.

The COUNTY OF LINLITHGOW was sold many times, the first time in 1905, and later she sailed under several different flags. In 1920 she was converted into a motorship, and in 1929 she was registered at Piraeus under the name KATHERINE.

To enable pilots to meet an incoming ship at sea, they have their own powered vessels stationed outside the entrance to all important ports. In earlier days, sailing vessels were used as pilot ships. The types varied considerably (see, for instance, Figure 25). Around the East Coast ports of the United States, especially New York, one encountered American pilot schooners of the type shown in Figure 42. The hull was always painted black and was copper sheathed, and its fine lines went back to the Baltimore clipper. The rigging characteristically had a large jib and no fore-topmast. In a gale, these schooners could lie to under the foresail only, close-reefed if necessary. The famous racing schooner AMERICA—the winner, in 1851 of the cup later named after her—was modeled on the lines of New York's pilot schooners. The development of pleasure yachts for racing or cruising was a process of refining the lines and equipment of the agile and powerful pilot vessels and fishing schooners.

MACFIE

43

American bank schooner, knockabout type, ETHEL B. PENNY

From the same band of shipbuilders came the American fishing schooner, which came to be called the "Gloucester schooner"; it was used for fishing on the Newfoundland banks and hailed from the ports in the Down East states. The Gloucester schooner was built with a deep keel, fine lines, and had a large sail plan, with well-made fore-and-aft sails.

Originally, these schooners were rigged with a long jibboom and a large jib, which was always difficult to furl in bad weather. The bowsprit was referred to as the "widow-maker." In port the long jibboom was in the way, and in 1901 McManus built a schooner with a long overhang forward and without a jibboom. This new type of schooner was called the "knockabout," and at first she had few followers; but later she became very popular, and when fishing schooners were generally equipped with oil engines, about 1916, the type prevailed.

Figure 43 shows the bank schooner ETHEL B. PENNY, of Gloucester, Massachusetts. Her hull and rig are characteristic of these beautiful fishing schooners. The graceful bow of the Gloucester fisherman is more than an extension of the hull forward to incorporate the bowsprit, making the fore-triangle inboard. Previously, all sailing craft had either the plumb bow (a vertical stem) or the clipper bow (a concave stem). With the knockabout bow, called the "spoon bow," when a vessel heeled down, her waterline increased in length, and she was capable of greater speed. The principle involved is that a sailing ship has a top speed, called "hull speed," that is a function of her displacement and her length on the water. Hull speed is reached when water cannot be moved out of the way any faster to allow the craft to continue accelerating. All additional impetus from the wind in the sails is transformed into a bigger bow wave, the so-called bone in her teeth of a boat beating fast to windward. The spoon bow meant that although the displacement of the craft remained constant, she increased her length on the water when heeled down and so had greater potential speed. Further, below the waterline, Gloucester fishermen cut away the forefoot, the area of the hull where the stem meets the keel, to lighten the displacement and provide a more rounded shape that would remain symmetrical underwater even when one side of the boat was higher out of the water than the other.

Nathaniel Herreshoff, the famous American yacht designer, revolutionized racing sailing when, in 1891, he built GLORIANA, the first yacht with a spoon bow (she also had a bowsprit). So successful was this ship that naval architects immediately began copying her lines, and many older boats had their bows rebuilt.

The topmast stay of the ETHEL B. PENNY is set up at the stemhead, while the forestay is attached well aft of the stem. Between the masts, she carries a large main-topmast staysail, well-known as a "fisherman's staysail."

The port of London, as do all major ports, has its own local types of craft for varying purposes. The Thames barge, Figure 44, is one well-known type. It is straight-stemmed, has a square stern and a shallow draft, and is flat-bottomed, enabling it to sit comfortably on the bottom when the tide is low. It can sail with less leeway because it has leeboards similar to those of the Dutch bolter. It has a deck with a large hatch amidships, and right astern is a cabin below the low quarterdeck. Usually rigged ketch-fashion, it has a large spritsail, which is furled with brails, a topsail, two or three headsails, and a small mizzen that always has the sheet on the rudder, so that when the rudder is put to leeward, the mizzen sheet is payed off as well. The Thames barge is one of the few older types of small local vessels that still exist.

On the other hand, the English sailing trawler, the fishing smack that worked the various fishing ports of Great Britain, has entirely disappeared. At the end of the last century, these vessels were so numerous that they formed a floating town on the fishing banks in the North Sea, a town with a floating church, a floating store, where payment was made in fish, and a floating pub, where the same currency was valid, and with the fishermen's own organized buyers, who took the fish ashore, so that the ships could remain at sea for long periods. Figure 45 shows such a typical fishing smack, the HOME SECURITY, BM 67, of Brixham. The hull has the traditional cutter form, with a straight stem, a well-modeled counter, and

a deep keel. The ketch rig has an almost horizontal jib-boom, a main topmast, but a pole mizzenmast. Fishing vessels are still registered in special registers kept by the respective county administrations. The marking consists of the first and last letter of the place of registration and a number; the majority of European nations register their fishing vessels in this way.

Toward the end of the last century, English shipowners scrapped or sold the majority of their sailing ships, and very few new ships were built. It was mainly the French and the Germans who still built new sailing ships or, together with the Norwegians, bought up English second-hand tonnage. The French subsidized their sailing ships, but they as well as the Germans tried to make them pay by building large ships complete with water-ballast tanks and a highly mechanized rig.

As early as the 1870's, the largest ships were rigged with double-topgallant yards, designed in the same way as the double-topsail yards. Then, after a first short trial in 1875, a ship was rigged in 1887 with double-topgallant yards and without royals, and the topgallant sails were made somewhat deeper. Since 1887 was the jubilee year of Queen Victoria, for many years this mode of rigging was called "jubilee rig." Later, seamen called such a ship "bald-headed" or a "stump topgallant yarder." However, this economic rigging was not to become general, and the last large sailing ships were all rigged with double-topgallant yards and royals. In these large ships, wire was used to a large extent for the running rigging, hal-

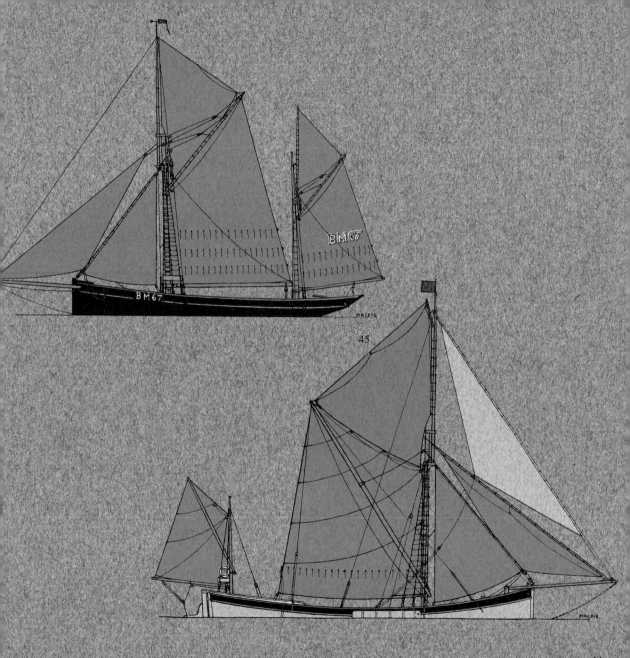

BM67

BM 67

MACFIE

45

MACFIE

44

MAGPIE

46

yards, braces, downhauls, and clew lines; even buntlines were made of flexible wire.

Because the large ships had a relatively lower rig and longer yards, all sails were broad but not deep, and the method of clewing up sails was changed so that they were clewed up to the yardarms instead of to the bunt (or to the middle of the yard).

Some of the largest sailing vessels built around the turn of the century were rigged with five masts. The first of these was built in 1890 for French shipowners, closely followed by just as large a vessel for German shipowners. Both these ships were built in Scotland; but in 1895, Tecklenborg's shipyard in Geestemünde built the largest sailing ship in the world, which was rigged as a five-masted bark and was named POTOSI. The owner was Herr Ferdinand Laeisz of Hamburg. All ships owned by Laeisz had names beginning with the letter "P," and they were known by sailors the world over as good, efficient, and well-kept vessels.

The Laeisz P-line had begun in the 1870's with a few small vessels. From the start, they made voyages to the west coast of South America, often carrying coal on the outward passage and saltpeter on the homeward journey. In 1892 this firm built two four-masted barks, both of 2,900 gross tons. Three years later they built the large five-master POTOSI, of 4,026 gross tons, of 3,854 net register tons, and of 6,000 tons deadweight. The POTOSI had the following registered dimensions: length, 360 feet; beam, 49 feet; and depth of hold, 28 feet. The mainmast was 206 feet high from the deck, and she carried a total of 24 square sails and 18 fore-and-aft sails. The largest ship of this line—and probably the largest sailing ship ever constructed—was the PREUSSEN. She had five masts also and was ship-rigged.

Figure 46 shows the POTOSI with a high forecastlehead, a bridge deck amidships, and a small poop aft. On the bridge deck, we can see the chart room, forward of which stands the steering wheel, as the vessel was steered from amidships. The rig has double-topgallant sails and royals, that is, six square sails on each mast. On the fifth mast, the jiggermast, the POTOSI has two gaffs, and thus the large spanker is divided in two.

All the square sails are clewed up to the yardarms, and short gaskets direct the clew lines to the leech of the sails. The upper topsail yards have double lifts, and note that both the topsail and the topgallant downhauls are shackled to the clew of the sails instead of to the yard below. This was an aspect of German rig that was never copied by the English. Its advantage was that when the upper yard was lowered, the downhaul served as a clew line and lifted the clew of the sail up toward the yard as far as the sheet of the sail allowed, and thus the sail was easier to furl.

The topsails as well as the topgallant sails were hoisted with hand winches. The halyards were therefore made of wire, and they led directly, without tackles, to the drum of the halyard winch, the gain in power being obtained through a worm gear. The braces were also maneuvered with winches, and one brace winch served each mast. The brace winch was ingeniously constructed. Three shafts connected with cogwheels, and each shaft was fitted with two drums. Each of the braces of the three lower yards led to one shaft, so that the starboard and port braces had one drum each. When the winch was turned, the braces on one side rolled off at the same pace as the braces on the other side rolled on, and the yard could be placed at any angle to the wind. The three upper yards always had ordinary hauling braces made of wire with Manila falls. The brace winch was constructed toward the end of the 1890's by the Scots sea captain J. C. B. Jarvis, and while it never became widespread in English ships, the Germans and the French introduced it in all their large vessels in this century.

The brace winches were of great assistance, for they made it easier to brace the heavy yards in bad weather. With a deadweight cargo, freeboard was low, and with brace winches fitted on the center line, there was less danger of the crew's being washed overboard in heavy weather than there was when the seamen worked the old type of braces at the bulwark.

In many ports, mostly in America, there were lighters—ships used to unload larger vessels at a mooring—built almost like boxes. When they had decks, the cargo was placed there, and they were used for occasional transport of plain goods, even of garbage. They were internationally known as "scow schooners" or "scows," and since they were built of straight timber and joined at right angles, they could be built without any specialized knowledge of shipbuilding. This is probably the reason why even small sailing vessels long ago were built in a boxlike manner; such ships were found in most countries where there had been extensive immigration. These small scows were seen on the Great Lakes of North America, on the West Coast of the United States, and in Australia and New Zealand.

Figure 47 shows a scow from New Zealand. She has perfectly straight sides and a flat bottom, and the bows are brought together like a snowplow. To enable her to sail by the wind, she was furnished with a centerboard in a trunk amidships that could be lowered and raised with the assistance of a winch. On deck she has a deckhouse and a cabin. Her only boat hangs in fixed davits athwartships over the stem. She is rigged as a ketch and has the traditional rig, with a boom under the foot of the forestaysail. Of special interest are the somewhat unusual lines fitted on the lifts of the gaffsails. They served to catch the sails when they were lowered. In the English-speaking sailing world, these lines were known as "lazy jacks," and they were also common in large American schooners.

MACRIE

47

MAGPIE

48

In the days of sail, many Scandinavian sailors voyaged down under in these small vessels. Others stayed at home on the Baltic and sailed in similar small craft. Figure 48 shows us a two-masted fore-and-aft schooner from the Åland Islands. She was employed in ordinary coastal trade in the northern Baltic and the Gulf of Finland. She was not very big and was always sailed by two or three men.

The rig had standing gaffs with brails in the sails, and for beating and going about in the narrow channels of the Baltic archipelagoes, there were often no stays between the masts, so that the topsails of the mast forward did not have to be shifted for different tacks. The after gaff had ordinary vangs, while the forward gaff had only one vang, which led to the crosstrees of the after-mast. Long ago, when there was no central heating, one important service performed by the Åland schooners was to bring firewood to Stockholm, and they often filled the quay on Strandvägen, the main avenue along one of the waterways in Stockholm.

The skillful Norwegian shipbuilder Colin Archer, who in 1892 built Nansen's famous polar exploration vessel, the FRAM, also built improved types of pilot boats, fishing boats, and sailing lifeboats. In 1893 he designed his first *livredningssköite,* on behalf of the Norwegian Lifesaving Association. This vessel, which was the first cruising lifeboat in the world, went to sea in all weathers, or, rather, she left port when a storm was brewing in order to assist any mariner in need of help. As a result of her excellent sailing qualities, she had many successors, and this was one of the reasons why the Norwegian Lifesaving Association retained sailing lifeboats without engines longer than other nations. Colin Archer's lifeboat, which carried his name, is shown in Figure 49. Her lines were something like those of a modern Scandinavian *kosterbåt.* She had low deck erections and was ketch-rigged, which is very well suited for cruising in bad weather, the mizzen tending to act as wind shadow on the main; also, in heavy winds, a ketch rig enables the mariner to drop the mainsail and sail on jib and jigger alone.

Lifesaving organizations have an old tradition, especially in England, where lifesaving stations were established in dangerous waters as early as the end of the eighteenth century. These stations were equipped with mortars that fired a lifeline to a stranded ship. Later, land-based lifeboats were also used, the majority being rowboats that went to sea when a ship needed assistance. Later came lifeboats with sails, but now only engine-driven craft are used. These vessels are self-righting, and their engines are constructed so as to operate even if entirely immersed.

Figure 50 shows an English lifeboat, constructed about the turn of the century by the famous yacht builder C. L. Watson. The Royal National Lifeboat Institution, which maintains the numerous English lifesaving stations, is entirely supported by voluntary contributions.

The Swedish offshore fishing industry was gradually developed from the early methods used in shore fishing, and as early as the eighteenth century, fishermen from the county of Bohuslän fished with so-called bank smacks on the rich fishing banks in the North Sea and off the Norwegian coast. Toward the middle of the nineteenth century, the bank smacks began to be replaced by more seaworthy decked vessels called "sea boats." These were generally carvel-built, though some clinker-built vessels also existed. Their approximate dimensions were: length, 46 to 53 feet; beam, up to 19 feet. They were ketch-rigged and very seaworthy. Figure 51 shows one of these sea boats, the VIKINGEN, from Gullholmen, circa 1880. Sweeps for auxiliary use lie in two crutches by the gunwale between the masts. She has a long jibboom, an outrigger astern for the mizzen sheet, loose-footed gaff-sails, and large trapezoidal topsails.

Every sea boat had a dinghy that was clinker-built, double-ended, very beamy relative to its length, and seaworthy. The fishing lines were trawled from the dinghy while the sea boat lay at anchor.

Among local types of small vessels that developed in Nordic waters, there was none more prominent than the craft from the Roslagen area in the Stockholm archipelago. There were two main types: the smaller, called a SANDKIL (the word is philologically related to "keel"), was rigged with a staysail and a hoisting mainsail; the larger, a sloop, was rigged with a standing gaff, topsail, staysail, and jib. Both had clinker-built hulls with carvel-built topsides. They were only partly decked and had a large open hatch amidships. The *sandkil* had accommodations built into the stem below a low half deck, while the sloop was equipped with a small deckhouse aft. These craft were always sailed by two men only, and it was an old rule that the earnings were divided into three equal parts, of which the vessel, the owner, and the mate received one part each. In this way, the skipper did not receive larger wages per se than the hired mate. The work was equally shared, and each worked as hard as

50

51

54

the other with the cargoes and sails; and if the voyage was successful, the skipper made money on his vessel.

Figure 52 shows the last Roslagen sloop, built in 1921 north of Stockholm and called GRETA-LINNEA. She sailed for only a few years, after which she was equipped with an oil engine and used as a motor barge. The rig is of special interest; she has a standing gaff, and when furled, the mainsail was brailed in to the mast. The topsail was always carried on one side and was never shifted from port to starboard, and the shrouds were rattled down only on the same side as the topsail. However, there were no definite rules for this; some sloops had a starboard topsail, others had a portside topsail. In the picture, the GRETA-LINNEA has a portside topsail. The forestaysail sheet was always a chain, loosely reeved through the clew of the sail and thus serving as a horse at the same time. This steadied the staysail when the vessel went about. The picture shows the GRETA-LINNEA with a cargo of firewood, bound for Stockholm. Because she sailed in the sheltered water of the archipelago, she carried huge deckloads. A few reef points were tied in the staysail so the sail would not be chafed by cargo.

In Norway, with her deep fjords and where road transport is often difficult, coastal shipping has always been important to communications. Since the Viking Age, the square sail has been predominant among Norwegian fishing vessels and coastal craft; and at an early date, local vessels were developed, every large fjord having its own type. This small one-masted vessel was known as a "yacht"—or, rather, many different local craft were known under the same name. On the Baltic, the yacht was fore-and-aft-rigged and had a bowsprit and staysails.

Figure 53 shows a trading yacht from Nord Fjord, southwest of Ålesund. Her dimensions are: length, 64 feet; beam, 29 feet. With her strong, clinker-built broad hull and sharp ends, she had plenty of buoyancy but still sailed well. The high stem is a survival from the longships of the Viking Age. A cabin is built into the after end of the hull, and there is a small rail around

the deck on top. The mast was very tall, probably as much as 90 feet, with a deep sail crowned by a small flying topsail. The illustration was sketched from the last sailing yacht of this type, which was withdrawn from trading and is now preserved in the local museum at Nord Fjord.

The more the power-driven vessels were brought to perfection, the more uneconomical the sailing ships became, and after the turn of the century, only a few deepwater ships were built. Occasional booms made them pay temporarily, but the number of sailing vessels decreased yearly, and the few that were built were often experiments to try out a simpler rig that would require a smaller crew and thus mean less expensive upkeep. In 1904, two four-masted barkentines were built in Greenock for German shipowners. They were called BEETHOVEN and MOZART, each of 2,005 gross and 1,877 net register tons, with registered dimensions of 260 by 40.5 feet. They were up-to-date vessels with water-ballast tanks; they had practical rigging with halyard winches and brace winches, a donkey engine for the deck machinery, and double-topgallant yards on the square-rigged foremast. The BEETHOVEN had a short life, but the MOZART survived the First World War, belonging to Hamburg until 1922, when she was sold to Hugo Lundquist, who was the great shipowner of Mariehamn before Gustaf Erikson. This vessel was broken up in 1936.

Figure 54 shows the MOZART under full sail. This drawing is our first and only figure that shows double-topgallant yards without royals. The lower topgallant yard is trussed to the topmast cap, and the lower topsail yard is trussed to the lower cap; above, the upper topgallant yard is hoisted on the topgallant mast, the upper topsail yard on the topmast. The brace winch for the heavy yards was placed in front of the mainmast, but it is not shown in the picture. The spike bowsprit is decorated with a shark's tail as a sign that she is sailing in deep water and perhaps also as a charm. A lee-side lifeboat is seen sailing just ahead of the MOZART.

The most important coastal sailing vessel of the southwestern Baltic was developed in the waters around Schleswig-Holstein and the Danish islands. This formerly very common craft is also called a "yacht." The hull has a curved stem without a figurehead, a square stern without counter, and a rudder abaft everything. Until about 1870 the cabin was built belowdecks with windows in the square stern, but later the cabin was placed higher and detached from the stern, especially in larger vessels. As the hull of this yacht was seaworthy and practical, two- and three-masted schooners were also built on similar lines. This shipbuilding school was concentrated around the Danish island of Aero and the town of Marstal, and all vessels with a similar hull were referred to by Scandinavian sailors as "marstal-built."

Figure 55 shows such a marstal yacht from the turn of the century. She had a strong hull, was often built of oak and beech, and was very seaworthy. In the picture, she is rigged with a trapezoidal topsail and sets a flying square sail on the lower mast. When this sail was furled, the upper yard was lowered onto the lower and the gaskets were taken around both the yards and the sail.

MACEJE

55

MACFIE

56

Swedish three-masted topsail schooner RAGNAR, *built in 1916. "I sailed as a deck boy in the* RAGNAR *in 1926"* — *Gordon Macfie*

Figure 56 shows a larger vessel of the same type, here rigged as a three-masted topsail schooner. She was, however, not built in Denmark but in Sweden, namely, in 1916 at Viken, north of Hälsingborg. She was called RAGNAR and was built for owners in Hälsingborg. With dimensions of 105 by 26 by 10.3 feet, she was of 198 gross and 172 net register tons and was able to carry 350 tons deadweight. RAGNAR was one of the last sailing ships to be built in Sweden. The picture shows RAGNAR with double topsails and with a flying square sail hoisted under the foreyard. She has a long jibboom and bowsprit in the same spar to take three headsails. The hull has a nearly straight stem without a figurehead, and the dinghy is slung in davits athwartships over the stern. On deck she has a forecastle and galley built into the deckhouse by the foremast, and the cabin is sunk in the low poop deck aft. The vessel is painted white, and she had coal-tarred boat topping and red antifouling below the waterline.

The boom of the First World War still prevailed a few years after she was built, but during the lean years of the twenties, she, as well as so many others, sailed with little profit. In 1930 she was equipped with an auxiliary engine and was used during the years of economic depression. The artist Gordon Macfie, who illustrated this book, was fifteen years old when he sailed as a deck boy in the RAGNAR in 1926. The vessel voyaged to Höganäs three times that year to load bricks. These were loaded at a rate of 100 tons a day, and the whole cargo passed through his hands while he stood on deck catching the bricks in midair and passing them down the hold; the bricks were thrown aboard by trained stevedores from railway trucks on the quay. In the evenings, the young deck boy was so tired that he could neither eat nor undress. He fell asleep wet and dirty and was called to continue work each morning with a stiff body and sore hands. Ultimately, it is economy that regulates work, and the small vessels employed on the Baltic operated under very reduced circumstances. Young Gordon was paid about $9 per month.

The large deepwater sailing ships were no better off financially, and those that still existed in the postwar period decreased in number. Some foundered, but the largest decrease was due to scrapping, and only the best ships could continue to sail. Their continued voyages were a great achievement technically as well as economically. With small young crews, they sailed around the world on the outward passage to Australia and came home around Cape Horn. This required both skill and luck, for a lost suite of sails might mean financial ruin to a ship.

One of the last of these large vessels was the four-masted steel bark ARCHIBALD RUSSELL. She was built at Greenock in 1905 and was the last four-masted bark built for a British shipowner, J. Hardie & Co., Glasgow, who stuck to sailing ships to the last. In 1924 she was bought by Gustaf Erikson of Mariehamn, the only shipowner in the world who managed to make sailing ships

pay during the postwar period. In the summer of 1939, the ARCHIBALD RUSSELL arrived in Hull. Soon afterward, she was seized owing to the outbreak of war, during the course of which she was damaged. A few years later, she was broken up.

Figure 57 shows the ship as seen from the lee side. Note all the buntlines in the sail. The hull is that of the large sailing ships, with a high forecastlehead, termed a "topgallant forecastle," three deckhouses, a high poop, a chart room, and a wheelhouse of steel. The latter provided excellent protection for the helmsman when the ship was running before the wind in heavy weather. The ship is shown in her English garb; she has a painted-ports hull and is flying the English colors. The rig has double-topgallant sails and royals above the double topsails, and forward she has four headsails, namely, a fore-topmast staysail, an inner and outer jib, and a flying jib.

MACFIE

MACFIE

58

58. *Danish four-masted schooner* KAJ HVILSOM, *of Svendborg, built in 1918*

After the First World War, very few sailing ships were built. In 1926 the Germans caused some sensation by building a four-masted bark, the PADUA, which was the last of her kind to be built. She was built for Laeisz's Flying P-line and employed on the cruel road around Cape Horn, sailing outward with coal or coke and homeward with sodium nitrate. She was practically identical with PASSAT and PEKING, built in 1911, and with POLA, 1916, and PRIWALL, 1918, all built for Reederei Laeisz in Hamburg. The penultimate big sailing ship to be built was probably the Danish five-masted bark KØBENHAVN, built in 1921 by Ramage & Ferguson at Leith as a training ship for the East Asiatic Company, Ltd., in Copenhagen. She was lost after leaving Buenos Aires on December 14, 1928, bound for Melbourne. It is believed that she struck ice and foundered in the lonely and stormy Antarctic Ocean.

On the waterways of Western Europe, the auxiliary motor vessel took the place of the old sailing ships, and only a few small schooners were built. Figure 58 shows a Danish four-masted fore-and-aft schooner, built with fine lines and quite different from the hull of the marstal type of schooner. This clipperlike hull was common in the waters around the Danish island of Fyn and was known as a "Svendborg-built schooner." The picture shows the schooner KAJ HVILSOM, built in 1918 at Svendborg for owners in the same town. She still has a foreyard, below which a flying square sail is hoisted. When this was set, the forestaysail was hauled down, and its halyard was unshipped and used to hoist the square sail. Triangular topsails are set on the lifts of the yard. These topsails were one of the last innovations of the dying sailing ship, and they were never given a standard name. The KAJ HVILSOM was sold to Estonia in 1926.

59. *Swedish three-masted fore-and-aft schooner* DAGNY, *built in 1926, the last sailing ship to be built in Swede.*
60. *American six-masted schooner* WYOMING, *built at Bath, Maine, in 1909, of 3,730 gross tons, length 330 feet.*
was the longest wooden vessel in the worl

Figure 59 shows us another of these small Baltic schooners, the DAGNY. She was the last sailing vessel to be built in Sweden and was a three-masted fore-and-aft schooner, completed in 1926 at Ystad, Skåne. She has the hull of the marstal type, with a square stern and a nearly vertical curved stem. She was ordered as a pure sailing ship, but before she was launched, she was equipped with an auxiliary oil engine, and she was thus never a true sailer.

Apart from the large square-rigged ships, another class of sailing vessel was developed in the United States, the American schooners. Many of these were three- and four-masted, some five-masted, a few six-masted, and one alone seven-masted, the THOMAS W. LAWSON, built in 1902. These large schooners handled entirely differently from square-rigged ships, and a sailor who was used to square-riggers was never happy in a schooner. Most of the work took place with the assistance of steam winches, and steam from the donkey boiler was available the whole time the vessel was at sea. Naturally, the crew would hoist the large sails with the assistance of a steam winch, but, in addition, they hoisted and hauled down the staysails and clewed up the gaff-topsails with engine power. They even furled the large gaffsails with the assistance of the steam winch. The lines running vertically from the lifts, called "lazy jacks," served this purpose. The lee-side lift was well overhauled when the gaff was lowered, so that the large sail mostly lay on deck inside the lee-side lazy jacks. The sail was stretched out and smoothed on deck; the tackle fall of the lee-side lift was then taken to the winch and heaved in. The lazy jacks slowly raised and rolled the sail up toward the boom, so that when the two lifts were evenly taut and all lazy jacks stretched, the sail lay rolled horizontally between the latter and vertically between the boom and the gaff.

Figure 60 shows the six-masted schooner WYOMING, built in Bath, Maine, in 1909 for owners in New York. She was the longest wooden ship ever built, being no less than 330 feet long, surpassing the large clipper GREAT REPUBLIC by a couple of yards.

The WYOMING was shelter-decked and had an open rail along the whole length of the side. She had several steam winches on deck, and the deckhouses were built on the main deck, so that only half of the erections extended above the shelter deck, making the houses as low as the rail. The six masts were the fore, main, mizzen, jigger, driver, and spanker. The aftermost gaffsail in all these schooners, with the exception of a two-master, was always called the "spanker." The size of the WYOMING is perhaps best understood from the information that her spanker boom was 90 feet long and was so thick that when a tall, long-legged man sat astride it, his feet did not show below the boom. To run before the wind, to scud, or veer in a gale, or to jibe these enormous gaffsails was almost fatal, and anyone who experienced it longed to be on board a square-rigged ship, which with yards braced square ran safely before wind and sea.

MACFIE

59

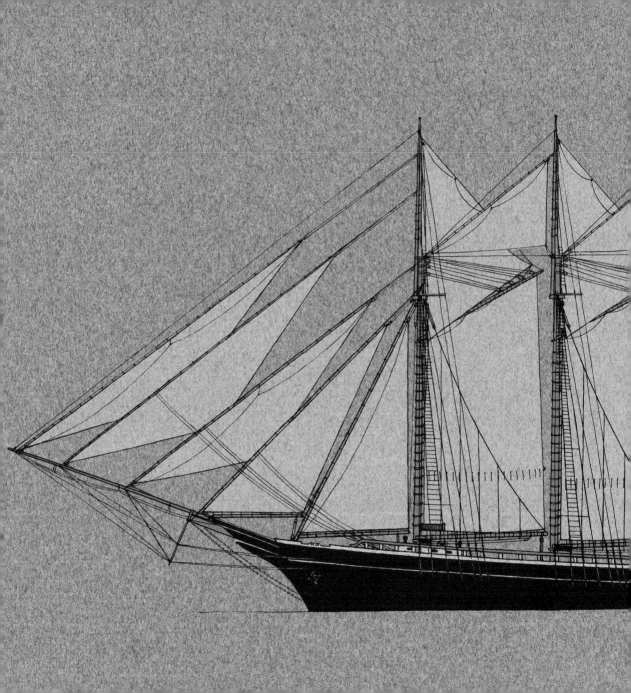

As sailing ships became fewer, interest in them grew, and in some parts of the world the last ships were preserved in museums. The CUTTY SARK, a China clipper of fame, built in 1869, is preserved at Greenwich. In the Medway, the ARETHUSA, the ex-German four-masted bark PEKING, is a training ship. At Travemünde, the PASSAT is kept as a stationary training ship, and so is the VIKING, at Göteborg. In Mariehamn, the POMMERN is annexed to the local shipping museum; in San Francisco, the BALCLUTHA, an old steel ship built in Glasgow in 1886, is restored to her old glory; the CHAPMAN lies permanently moored in Stockholm harbor and is used as a youth hostel; in Mystic, Connecticut, the whaler CHARLES MORGAN, her keel fixed in cement, is the prime attraction of the restored nineteenth-century port. In the summer of 1964, a race was organized from Lisbon to Bermuda for the tall ships still maintained by maritime powers as training ships. From Bermuda, many of these vessels, representing Germany, Denmark, Argentina, Portugal, Norway, and the United States, sailed into New York harbor, their high rigs an unbelievable sight against the city's skyscrapers.

Apart from these and a few more relics of the past, the sailing ship is no more, and no cargoes are transported today across the sea by the wind. After thousands of years of trading along shore and hundreds of years of sailing in deep water, man has turned his mind to other sources of power, mainly oil; and all over the world, countless natural wind forces are unused for any practical marine purpose.

The vignette opposite is a drawing of the figurehead that adorned the bark BEATRICE, from Göteborg.

The sailor of old, whose ability to foretell wind and weather determined the success of his voyage, who knew everything about ropework, who handled his sails with great skill by night or day, blow high or low, has gone the way of his ship. His art is lost, and before long it will be a task for sociologists to try to find out and describe how a seaman worked his ship across the sea with only God's wind for driving power.

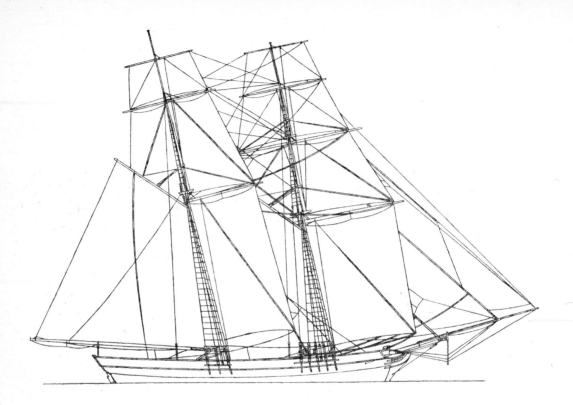

The DOS AMIGOS was a ship with a truly remarkable history. In the late 1820's, the British were able to capture a very speedy slaver-brig. The vessel was purchased into the Royal Navy and employed on slaver patrol under the interesting sobriquet the BLACK JOKE. One of the slave vessels in turn captured by the BLACK JOKE was the DOS AMIGOS, which was also purchased into the Royal Navy and was rechristened the FAIR ROSAMOND. The DOS AMIGOS was a perfect example of a class of slaving ship designed to meet the special requirements of that nasty business. Small, exceedingly fast, she had sufficient capacity to carry enough slaves to turn a profit after expenses.

The rig was an important consideration for the designer.

Often the choice was between the schooner rig and the brig. Brigantine and hermaphrodite rigs also were used. Of course, all slavers carried square sails, as befitted a ship that would be a deepwater sailer. The DOS AMIGOS represented the most popular size of schooner-slaver. After becoming the FAIR ROSAMOND, her rig was cut down. While this work was being done, a drawing of her original rig was made. The figure above represents the sail plan she used while in the slave trade. She was built for speed, largely because of the high mortality rate among the slaves and the fact that profit hinged on the delivery of a live cargo. The great spread of sails indicates that she held up well in a squall but was also able to make speed in light and moderate weather.

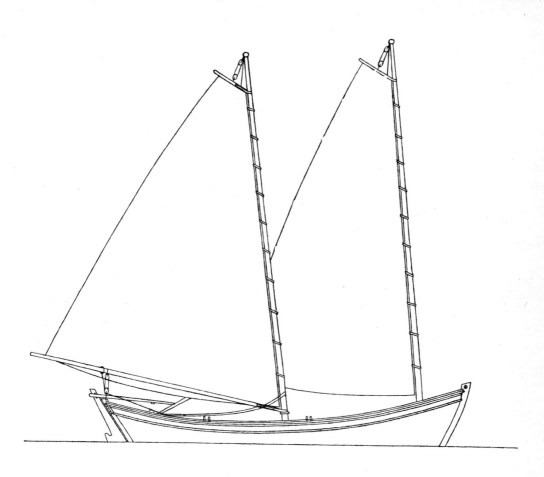

The Block Island cowhorn was one of the best known of all the American beach boats. It had a fine reputation for safety and appears to have gotten its nickname from some fancied resemblance of the boat's profile to a pair of horns. These boats ranged in length from 17 to about 40 feet and came into use some time after 1840.

The boat was rigged as the old shallops were, with some modifications. There were two slightly raked masts, the main located about midship, the foremast well forward in the boat. The foresail was loose-footed and overlapped the main. No light sails or jibs were carried. The cowhorn was originally designed for two men for fishing in open waters in any sort of weather. Modern versions of this boat have found great use in a variety of weather conditions. American yachtsmen have become quite familiar with this design with modifications.

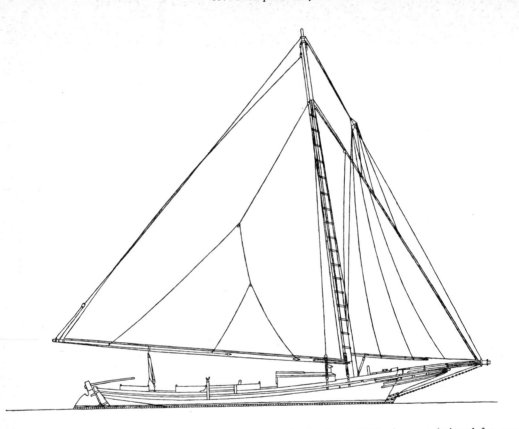

One of the boats most commonly associated with the Chesapeake was the skipjack, more frequently known as a "bateau." These ranged in size from 22-footers to huge sloops of about 60 feet in tonnage length. Most of these bateaux were jib-and-mainsail-rigged. The rake of the masts in all varieties of bateaux was severe. The larger boats were decked with a trunk aft and a forecastle hatch forward. The smaller boats were decked with a small trunk forward. The very smallest were half-decked for tonging or dredging oysters or for crabbing.

A subclass consisted of the "oyster pirates," and the figure above shows a boat originally built for poaching purposes. When her "pirate" days were over, she was sold and used as a pleasure boat. Built near Oriole,

Maryland, about 1900, she was designed for speed, in order to avoid capture, but was also massive enough to withstand the enormous strain of hauling the dredge and carrying heavy rig in bad weather. These boats usually had well-cut sails and were fitted with lazy jacks, a device that enabled poachers to lower sails quickly without resorting to furling. The large sail area on a rather low rig enabled these boats to move well in light weather, but they were surprisingly seaworthy and were able to withstand rough seas extremely well. Of course, reefing was necessary in a strong wind because of the large sail area, and the jib was usually taken in under such conditions, for the boats hauled their dredge most efficiently with a strong weather helm.

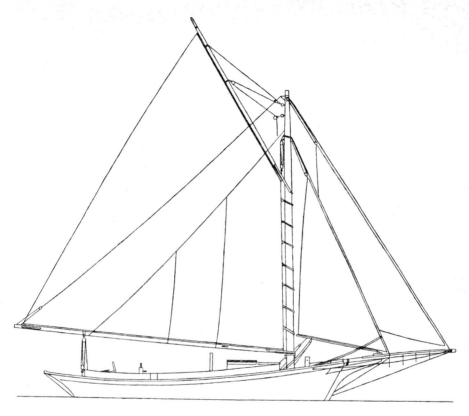

One of the most interesting American designs was the Friendship sloop, a type of sloop built on Muscongus Bay in Maine, in and around the town of Friendship, which gave its name to the design. It was also known as the "Morse sloop," after the family whose excellent boats were widely known. This sloop was a jib-and-mainsail boat, the larger ones carrying a gaff-topsail and, usually, a jib topsail as well. The smaller version of the Friendship sloop had no topmast or gaff-topsail. The three lowers constituted their sails. Many of these boats could be handled with a triple-reefed mainsail alone, though a headsail was carried in the event that the craft would be called upon to tack often or would be making a passage in narrow or dangerous waters.

The keel sloop of the present Friendship style of hull made its appearance in the late 1880's, and the model became very popular among New England's lobster fishermen. And, inevitably, because of the ruggedness and sailing ability of the boat, yachtsmen began to copy the design. By the late 1890's a yachtsman could purchase a 25-foot sloop for $675. When a Muscongus Bay sloop was converted, it was the usual procedure to dock her main boom and shorten the bowsprit a bit. The result was that sail area was lost, and therefore the boat neither sailed as fast nor tacked as readily as before. True yachtsmen have deplored the fact that so many of these fine and powerful sloops were spoiled in an effort to make them cruisers that could be "easily" handled.

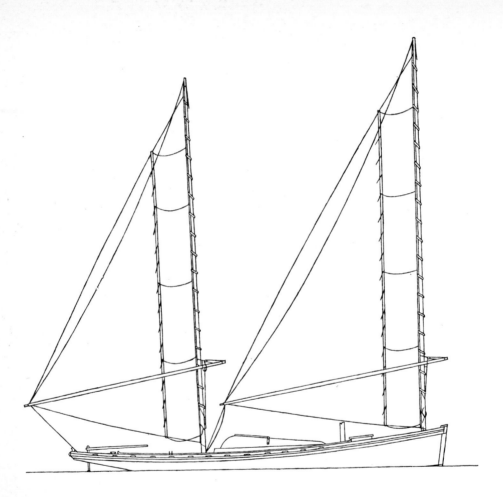

The earliest model of the New Haven sharpie is shown above (Figure 65). This two-masted vessel was apparently developed primarily as an oyster-tonging boat; it had the qualities of reasonable carrying capacity, steadiness, and low cost. The origin of the New Haven sharpie is unknown, though the boat was most popular in the fisheries at New Haven, Connecticut, in the 1870's.

The two-masted rig of the sharpie consisted of two leg-of-muttons, each with a sprit boom, as shown in the figure. The foresail sheet was in two parts, like separate jib sheets. The sails seem to have been laced to the masts in the early versions, but later on, mast hoops were used. The two-masted sharpies were always built with three mast steps, with one well forward for the foremast. When one man worked the sharpie, she was usually fitted with one mast.

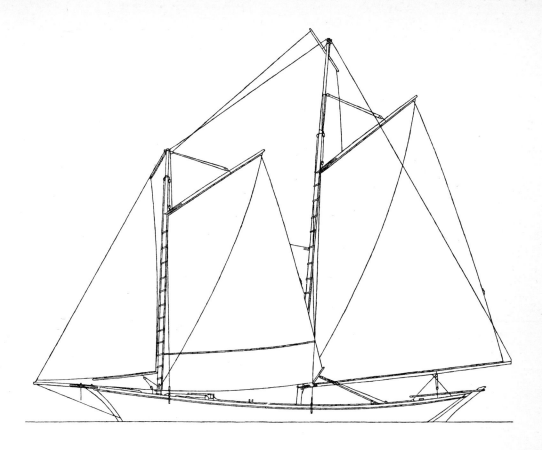

Nova Scotia contributed one of the best of the larger boat designs in the double-ended Tancook whaler. These were boats introduced in the 1860's, with one of the first apparently built at Lunenburg. The boat proved popular, and other models were then built at Tancook Island. Though the early models were no more than 30 feet in length, some of the later adaptations reached a length of nearly 50 feet. By about 1900, the boat design was thoroughly refined. The boat's lines were sharp, and sitting low in the water it had a most comely sheer. It was certainly one of the handsomest double-enders.

The rigging of this boat was a simple one, designed for maximum power. In a strong wind, the boat worked under a foresail or with a full mainsail and jib. If these arrangements proved to offer too much sail area for weather conditions, the sails were reefed. In light going, a supplementary main staysail was used. This became known as the "fisherman's staysail."

Because the Tancook whaler had such excellent sailing qualities, attempts were made to copy the hull design. But, as is usually the case, compromises and departures were made that led to a less than successful new boat.

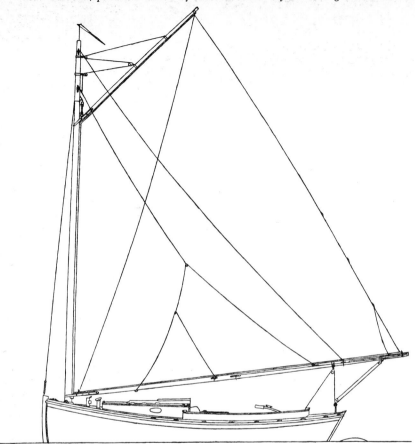

The Martha's Vineyard catboat, a model of which is shown above, is typical of the catboats that plied the waters of Massachusetts Bay and navigated along the shores of Cape Cod during the 1880's. Built at such ports as Plymouth and, later, in Boston harbor, these "cats" were used by lobster fishermen and also by solitary fishermen using handlines. The primary considerations in design were safety and ease of handling. Rigs were fitted carefully so that the proper gear would be at hand for the quick reefing of sails. The rig of a 20-foot catboat of this style usually called for a mast of about 27 feet, a boom of 24 feet, and a gaff of 11 feet. The sail area thus produced was about 350 square feet. These boats were powerful enough to operate in exposed waters, and in expert hands they could come through heavy weather quite well. The cat rig was close-winded, and in light air it lacked the sail area to make great speed. This proved a failing when the rig was adapted for yachtsmen, and they made immediate demands that the sail area be increased for greater speed in light air. The result was a bastardization of the design, a great many capsizings, and a loss of popularity that the catboat never regained. But the original design is still looked on with favor by the discerning judge.

SHIP

A full-rigged ship was a vessel of at least three masts, all of which were square-rigged. Each mast, and almost invariably the mizzen, could also be fitted with a fore-and-aft trysail at the level of the course; the trysail on the mizzen was referred to as the "driver" up to the middle of the nineteenth century, when it was then called the "spanker." A trysail abaft the fore- or mainmast was called a "spencer." On the mainmast, the sails from bottom to top were as follows: main course, or mainsail, main lower topsail, main upper topsail, topgallant, royal, skysail, moonraker. This last was rare. Together with staysails and studding sails, a full-rigged ship could carry more than an acre and a half of canvas. The record top speed for a clipper was 22 knots, and the record 24-hour run was 465 miles, an average of 19¾ knots.

BARK

A ship of at least three masts, of which the aftermost mast was fore-and-aft-rigged, the fore- and mainmasts square-rigged.

BARKENTINE

A three-masted (or more) vessel with the foremast square-rigged, the main and mizzen fore-and-aft-rigged.

BRIGANTINE

A two-masted vessel with the foremast square-rigged; the main was fore-and-aft-rigged on the main course but had square main topsails.

HERMAPHRODITE BRIG

A variant, but really a brigantine: the foremast was square-rigged, the main course and topsails fore-and-aft-rigged.

BRIG

A two-masted vessel, both square-rigged.

SCHOONER

Originally and typically, a two-masted ship with both fore- and mainsail rigged fore and aft. (There have been schooners with up to seven masts.) Topsails can be square-rigged or fore-and-aft-rigged. There are many variants: topsail schooners with square topsails, staysail schooners with the foresail tack secured at the foremast but the luff of the foresail running on the mainmast stay, etc. In most schooners, the mainmast is stepped approximately amidships and is the taller.

KETCH

A two-masted rig with the mainmast forward and the mizzen stepped forward of the aft waterline. The sails are fore-and-aft-rigged.

SLOOP

A single-masted boat with at least one jib. The mast is forward of midship.

CUTTER

A single-masted boat with the mast stepped farther aft than on a sloop and closer to midship. The rig includes double headsails, a jib, and a forestaysail.

YAWL

This rig is usually used aboard pleasure yachts and can really be regarded as a sloop with a mizzen jigger. This small mizzenmast is stepped aft of the rudderpost. The advantage of this rig is that it splits the mainsail into more easily handled areas. Splitting the rig is less efficient, but it allows a better balance to the sails.